Lets start off by introducing ı
christened Thomas William, boı
Hospital, Lambeth London, to ̲ ̲ ̲ ̲ (Brown is a
Christian name) and Thomas Edward, now you may think
that's where my Christian name came from? However my
Mother told me that my christian name was derived from St
Thomas's Hospital, and William from the ward name, she
explained that I was the first baby boy born on William ward
after it re-opened from bomb damage, well there was a war
going on.

In the year 2010 I reached the grand old age of seventy, and
looking back at my amazing job opportunities and work
experiences, plus listening to the lack of work for today's
young, who it is said and I quote "that in the future many of
these will leave school/education and eventually retire without
ever working" so I thought I'd put pen to paper, and record for
posterity so, that at least my descendants would perhaps we
able to gain an insight into what is was like to go to work and
provide for your family, whilst enjoying the experience, well
some times!

First of all before we start, let me make it clear that whilst
some of the jobs may not be in the correct order, every thing
that is in this book is the truth, the whole truth and nothing but
the truth.

I didn't have what you could call the best start in life, born at the start of the Second World War, our house was bombed when I was six months old, and we were left with nothing but the clothes on our backs, in fact my cot was a wooden draw taken from a chest of draws. I recall Mum telling me later, "That whilst the bombs were dropping, and all around us the houses and factories were being reduced to piles of rubbish, every few minutes she kept pinching me to make sure I was alive"

We had no choice but to depart to Stoke on Trent, where my Father originated from, I should add that although we lived in London, my Mothers home town was Newcastle upon Tyne, again recalling Mothers memories, after the bombing raid finished she made her way back to where our house had stood, and while we had been sheltering in the designated Air Raid Shelters, looters had stripped the house of all its contents.

Mum or Mother, was as I've stated a Geordie woman, who stood for no nonsense off anyone, she met my Father and married him in London in 1938, at no time could you call it a marriage made in heaven, he was a Pastry Chef and my Mother was working in the hotel industry, as a chamber maid.

He was a hard drinking man, from a large family of six, four brothers Matt, John, Bill, Bart and two sisters, Anne and Kate, and according to mum all had drink problems except Anne.

When mum tried to call the marriage off, he threatened to commit suicide, so she felt sorry for him, and went ahead, but as mum said on many occasions "She went through hell and back many times, but at least she had her Boys" Her Boys, me and my brother Tommy, who was born in 1942; in fact she had four boys, one in 1939 who was stillborn, me 1940, Tommy 1942, and lastly one born in 1945 who had twisted limbs and died soon after birth.

You may have picked up on my name Thomas and my brother Tommy, he was in fact christened John Thomas, but like me his second name was used.

Now to Mum, she came from a what you would describe as a middle class family, her Father was a Blacksmith with his own business on Newcastle Docks, her Mother had never worked, she also had a sister, Janet but preferred the name Jean, and a brother Tom, her Mother (my Gran) would by today's standards be called a snob, she never accepted my Mother's marriage. As in her opinion her daughter had married beneath herself, and she never forgave her, yes, they maintained contact and spoke occasionally, but her other daughter, Jean, married Robert Hall (Bobby), a teacher, who became a Headmaster. He in fact went on to become the Chairman of the British Headmasters Association, so as you can imagine Jean was the centre of attention. Her son became a plasterer and lived in a council house with his Welsh wife, Olwyn, so again another disappointment.

My first experience of work started when I was very young, probably when I was about seven or eight. To earn pocket money I had a home made wooden cart and would go round the neighbours collecting their waste food, potato peelings, greens and bread, which I would then sell for coppers to allotment holders to supplement the feed of their hens and pigs. I then went on to helping the local stick man, this was selling sticks from a horse and cart, then, helping the local milkman, Reg Cooper, and as many as before me have done, became a paperboy.

I should mention that even at a very young age, probably as young as seven or eight, to have any chance of receiving coppers from my Father, we, my Brother and I, but because I was the oldest it was usually me, had to go out on to the streets collecting Fag ends, or as we called it, "Gutter Hole Flake". Our favourite haunt was at the back of the Bucknall Working Men's Club, at the rear of the premises they used to tip all the rubbish down an embankment; if we were challenged we would say we were looking for bottle tops.

I should mention that aged fourteen a friend and I opened a bicycle repair shop, it didn't last long, we fell out when a customer bought his bike in for repairs to the gears, Graham who was the repair man, wanted to charge half a crown (12.5p) where as I, the salesman, wanted to charge thirty bob (£1.50p) it must have been shortly after this I got myself a Saturday job, tea maker, errand boy, window cleaner & sweeper up at Blackwood's Pawn Brokers, Parliament Row, Hanley.

It's the 28th, June, 1955, it's my 15th, Birthday, and I've left school and ready to face the world!

Job 1 Blackwood's, Parliament Row, Hanley Pawnbrokers Assistant

Yes I've started working full time, it's a Tuesday and it's my birthday, at a weekly wage of two pound's and fifteen shillings (£2.75) per week, Two pound's, board, seventy five pence pocket money, and I had to pay my own bus fares!, so it was shanks pony. It was only about two miles each way, isn't it strange that two miles when you are young is nothing, now it's a marathon. I had been employed there as a Saturday worker for a few months. The first Monday came as a surprise to me, as my Uncle Bill was apparently a regular; his best suit was in on a Monday, out on a Friday.

This was the norm for a lot of people in the mid fifty's, and judging by the amount of Pawnshops that are now opening up, it appears that they are coming back into fashion, anyhow I'd only been there a couple of weeks when I had to be rushed into hospital as my appendix had burst, and I never went back, well window dressing and window cleaning was not really my forte.

Years later in answer to my grandchildren's question " Granddad what did you do when you left school?" when I told them that I'd worked in a Pawn shop, I could see the admiration in their eyes, I quickly explained it was Pawn not Porn, however my explanation of the sign hanging outside "Three Balls" didn't really help!

 Thinking back I didn't know what the word Porn stood for, until I was in my twenty's.

Job 2 J & G Meakin, Eagle Works, Ivy House Road, Hanley
Packer
This was in a Pottery firms dispatch warehouse. Bored by being off sick I went and got myself a job as a trainee packer.

Meakin's was at that time one of the areas leading pottery manufacturers, commonly called pot banks.
The job consisted of packing earthenware for export, I hadn't realised that the job entailed heavy lifting, which resulted in my stitches starting to open, so it was back on to the sick.

However I do recall have vague recollections that young boys and girls, were subjected to an initiation ceremony. This was a rather cruel practice, and could even be classed as sexual assault, it certainly would not be tolerated in today's society, I was however spared this ordeal, and no doubt it would have come later! They were just waiting for my health to improve!

There was a young girl there that had the nick name "Plastic Paps," apparently one day on her lunch break, she had been seen going in between the kilns with a male, on her return it was noticed that due to the heat from the kiln, when they had been amorous, her padded bra had become shall we say mis-shaped, hence the cry "Plastic Paps".

The other thing that will surprise you all, that in the short time I was there I was a offered a revolver with ammunition!, the seller assured me it worked, even offering to demonstrate, he claimed it was from the war, I didn't stay to find out!

Job 3 Taylor, Tunnicliffe & Co Ltd, Eastwood Works, Hanley.
Lodge Boy

Taylor & Tunnicliffe were manufacturers of ceramic electrical insulators, my duties included checking visitors into the factory, and either give them directions to the relevant department or if necessary escort them. My uniform was a Brown Slop, I also had to record vehicles weights and contents, both, on entering the factory and leaving, using the sites weighbridge. I remember at the job interview the comments that my first name was unusual, I'd spelt Thomas as Thosmos, I was that used to spelling my name as Thos William, anyway I still got the job.

Now it must have been about the third week in August, I know this because, the Potters holidays was always the last week in August. I was not entitled to any holiday pay, and was offered work at one of the Directors house's in Barlaston, I can't remember the house, but what stuck in my mind even at that tender age, was the class system. I was given work in the garden, I suppose I must have been supervised, but can't remember, except that I had to have my sandwiches along with a mug of Tea, sitting on my own, in the Greenhouse. Tender years, I can't believe I've used that expression; I was after all at that age a wannabe Teddy boy!

Job 4 National Coal Board: Hanley Deep Pit. Trainee Miner, Underground Haulage Hand,

First of all I had to undergo a training period which was split between Kemball pit, which was at Heron Cross, and Tunstall College. Kemball was besides being a coal producing mine, was also the local areas training pit and all trades had to attend. Tunstall was the academic side, plus it had gym facilities under the supervision of a ex Stoke City footballer, John McCue, who was mustard at throwing a medicine ball, especially if you weren't paying attention, which often applied to me.

Unfortunately I was rather accident prone, I can recall having my left hand crushed, and in another accident having my breastbone split. The area I was employed in was known as Ragman, my job on haulage was at the top of Ragman Dip, the job was to ensure the smooth running of the conveyer belt, the coal came up from the Coal face to where I was positioned, it then dropped on to a lower level belt, I had to ensure that no blockages occurred, also I had to look out for stones.

Another thing you had to be careful with, was seemingly innocent areas of coal dust, the miners on the coal face would drop their trouser and empty their bowels on to a shovel and throw it onto the belt, to be fair it was mainly the Poles and Czech's who were responsible. There was a story going around of such a thing happening, this lad had put his hand into what seemed like a pile of coal, realised what had happened, pulled his hand back rather sharply, cursing, and caught his hand on the wall, and without thinking did what was natural, sucked his injured fingers!

How true that is I don't really know, but it was certainly plausible, after all and this is true, if any really large lumps of coal were on the belt, you had to try and break it up, to make it more manageable, to do this, we used what was called a locker Pin, this was a metal bar that you placed into the wheels of the Pit Tubs, to act as a brake, any way this lad got a locker pin, and struck the lump of coal, and failed to move his other hand, the result, he lost two fingers.

On a lighter side, another one of the lads (who was a character with the ladies), was telling me one day of his problems, he told me that he'd got to get married, the problem was, which one, he's got two girls pregnant! He had several tattoos, this was in 1955, on his nipples he had the words Mild on one, and Bitter on the other, and on his belly button, it said Press for Hot Chocolate!

Lets talk about the area I worked in, Ragman, well, the bit I worked at was at the top of an incline, which was rather cool, not too hot & not too cold, however in the Potters holidays I worked in an area know as Tenfoot, this was very hot and lacking in air flow. The pits all suffered from vermin infestation, mice and cockroaches, this was from the days when Pit Ponies were kept down there, and they would have been brought into the pit via the fodder.

On the two week shutdown (Potters holiday), miners would place their unwanted sandwiches into empty pit tubs, the mice would scramble in after the food, but were unable to climb out. On the return to work it was common to find pit tubs with numerous dead mice in, some half eaten!

On the occasion I worked in this area, which was only a week, on the first day, come meal break, (snapping time) I had eaten my sandwiches, sat back and turned my helmet light off, thinking I'd have a twenty minute snooze, I felt a nip on my side, a mouse had nipped me. Talking about snapping, because of the heat and dust, you tended to try and take sandwiches that were moist, I told Mum of a rather unusual combination, cheese and jam, she gave it to me every day more or less, so I didn't dare make any more suggestions after that. I even knew of one miner who used to have kippers and jam! I never tried that. A common drink was cold tea in a bottle, I couldn't stand it! Another thing they used to do was chew tobacco, it kept your mouth moist, well that's what they claimed; I never tried it.

 My mind wanders to religion; firstly, let me explain the procedure of miners going down the Pit, at Hanley we had four deck cages, top deck standing, the other three decks sitting. There were two cages, side by side, but not necessary together. If you could, you tried to get into the top deck because in the lower decks you were subjected to whatever mischief those on the decks above you felt like, it was common to get a soaking, and it wasn't always water from the Miners water bottles; it was not unknown to be urinated on. You couldn't do a thing about it, by the time your deck was cleared for unloading, the culprits were gone. The cages were used mainly for coal tubs, and only used for the transportation of men at shift changeover time. Coal took preference to men at any other times, say a miner was injured, which often happened, the injured man had to be taken to number two shaft, which was some distance away and was a lot slower.

Anyway we come to the point of religion, I was on early shift, six till two, so it would be sometime before six a.m. As it happened I was on the top deck, what we didn't know was that over the weekend they had changed the wire rope that worked the cages. The Winder (man who operated the winding gear) decided to test the brake on the new wire rope, now, what you must bear in mind is that these cages travelled at a fast speed, your stomach turned until you were used to them, anyway he applied the brake, and our cage stopped suddenly, when I say stopped, that's not really the best way to describe stop, we were up and down as if we were on a piece of elastic, every thing went quiet, and every one, at least on the top deck was Praying, and bear in mind there would have been about 20 to 30 miners of all different nationalities. When we did land at the pit bottom, you wouldn't have thought that their prayers had been answered listening to the language, however the point is, in a crisis everyone prayed to their God.

I was attracted to the Pits because I claimed that my Mother was a Widow, which was a lie, but it allowed her the coal allowance, a ton and you only had to pay for the carriage. I say a ton, you in fact received 19 hundredweight, (cwt), one hundredweight was donated to the Coal Board's pensioners, but after the breastbone incident I decided it wasn't the life for me.

To finalise this part of my story I'll finish off telling you about the time I asked my Mum, if she could put me a curl into my hair, this style was the rage at the time, and was called a Tony Curtis. No problem, Mum bought a perming solution called, I believe it was called Twink, and promptly permed my hair, complete with curlers. I was up at four am to get ready for work, looked in the mirror and was horrified to see that I had a full head of tight curls, I washed it about three times, but it still looked the same.

I had to catch the pit bus at about 5-15 a.m. so I sneaked upstairs on the bus, with a hat pulled tightly on, hoping no one would notice, but to no avail, can you imagine the embarrassment of everyone shouting "Hey up lads we've got Shirley Temple on board," then joining in singing 'The good ship Lollipop"!, it took about a month before my hair restored to its natural self, and yes, I gave up on the Tony Curtis curl look!

Job 5 Lewis's Department Store, Lamb Street, Hanley Shop assistant

All the glamour and girls, I started there as a salesman in the glass & china ware department, that didn't last long, too many breakages, which resulting in me being transferred to the wood department. The one lasting effect my short stint in the china department had is here we are sixty years later, and I still have a longing and respect for Shelley Bone China. I was only fifteen, and because I had toothache, I had to go and see the nurse, she rubbed my gums with peroxide, and pointed out with great pleasure that my gums had gone white, she predicted that by the time I was twenty one I would have no teeth left, she explained that whiteness of my gums was the sign of Periodontitis, which is a disease of the gum causing the teeth to become loose, well I'm now seventy two, and even though I don't have a lot of teeth left, I certainly haven't suffered from gum disease, some would say I've worn them out with talking!

I recall a young girl workmate, similar age to myself, she was a very quiet girl, pretty and a redhead!, anyway she went pillion riding on a scooter to the seaside, but on the way they were involved in a collision, as was the norm in those days, crash helmets were not considered a necessity, she suffered head injuries, and has spent the rest of her life in mental institutions, so to any one reading this, take note, <u>Crash Helmets are essential.</u>

<u>Job 6 British Army, Malta Barracks, Aldershot Boy Soldier</u>
23246711, Royal Engineers, stationed at Malta Barracks, Aldershot, actually when I joined we were known as Boy Soldiers but it was changed to Junior Leaders whilst I was in. I signed on for nine years, in fact there was a couple of lads from Ireland who were only fourteen, at that time even though in England school leaving age was fifteen, in Ireland it was fourteen.

To join the Army you had to have a written exam, I had a hundred per cent pass mark. In the first week I was called to see our camp commander and was told that they were honoured to have me joining their ranks and that there was a great future for me, but that opinion didn't last long!

I think I spent the nine months I was there, in the Guard Room. My trouble centred on the fact that I thought I could take discipline, which at first was not a problem. The trouble started during our initial training, before joining up I had done a bit of boxing, anyway there was also another recruit who had a similar experience as myself in the ring, so the Army being brutal and having no regard to his weight against mine, matched us together.

Well as I was encouraged to do, I knocked him about, which in the Armies view was great, however this was alright until my opponent was promoted to Lance Corporal, that's when the rot set in. It was pay back time, or so he thought, I recall him ordering me to pull this handcart back to base, he ending with a bloody nose and sitting on the cart, and me under arrest!

This was the beginning of the end for William, so I decided to try and get a medical discharge, playing on a previous pit injury, I had had my left hand crushed, I claimed that as result I couldn't hold my rifle, well not hold it, more of I couldn't control the weapon on the recoil, on my appearance at the Medical Board, all seemed to be going well for me, until I was asked the question, did I like the Army life? I answered truthfully, "no" at that their attitude to me changed, and my application for a discharge was dismissed, so for me it was time to put my thinking cap on.

So it was back to normal and listening to the general sarcastic comments from the NCOs' on parade, like when they're standing behind you, and asking,

"Am I am hurting you laddie",

"No Sir",

"Well I bloody well should be, I'm standing on your hair get it cut," another one was, whilst shoving their face into yours,

"Had a shave?"

"Yes Sir,"

"Used a mirror,"

"Yes Sir,"

"Well use a bloody razor blade, they're sharper."

From there on things went rapidly downhill. I was on one occasion teamed with another recruit, Paddy McGill (a bit of a nutter), anyway we were on manoeuvres, and we had been dropped off in the middle of nowhere, equipped with maps, a small amount of food, a compass, sleeping bag and a tent. The food consists of dried powdered something, a couple of packets of biscuits, that were like dog biscuits, and a small amount of chocolate. We soon ate the chocolate and decided to catch the train and have a couple of days in his home town, Bognor Regis. We thought nothing could go wrong, which may have been correct, if Paddy hadn't got drunk, jumped off the pier fully clothed, lost his hat in the sea, and got arrested, so it was back to the Guard House.

To annoy the guards I stated my religion as Church of Scotland, this was because every Sunday you had to attend church, and being as you were under arrest, you had to have two guards escorting you, and I'd worked out that the Church of Scotland was two miles away from our barracks, and was the greatest distance away, if I was going to suffer so were they!.

At night you had a drink of cocoa before lights out at ten, mid morning at eleven o clock you had a break, a slice of bread, butter & jam and a mug of tea, however if, from the night before there was any cocoa left over, it was warmed up and served with the tea, it tasted vile, maybe it was because of the addition of Bromide, this is a chemical that is supposed to suppress your sexual urges, it must have been good stuff, for here we are nearly sixty years later and its working! This was served up in the NAAFI canteen, which was manned by civilians.

Moving onto manoeuvres, one such exercise was to run a few yards drop on to your stomach, roll over, crawl forward another few yards, then take a firing position, at this point along comes an NCO who inspects your rifle, now, in this ploughed field there was not a blade of grass to be seen, but guess what was in the barrel of my rifle, yep you're correct, grass! Yet another charge! Then, there was the time going over a ravine using your hands on a rope, carrying a bucket of water, the one who spilt the least was the winner. We were told, don't look down, I looked down, thought bloody hell, let the bucket go and used both hands, and another charge.

Some of the things they made you do, boarded on the ridiculous like painting coal white to match the snow, and cleaning the wooden floor with a toothbrush, you name I did it! One morning on parade we were all lined up for inspection, when the camp gorilla called Sergeant Major, bawled me out stating that I hadn't washed my neck etc, I was sent off on the double to get washed and then to report back to him, anyway, I went and had a read of a comic then back onto the parade ground for another inspection, this time the comments were "That's better."

Back to me and my attempt to get my medical discharge (working my ticket), I did all strange and weird things to convince them I was having trouble with my nerves, but not before I did a couple of runners, or as the army calls it, Absent With Out Leave, AWOL. The first time I got as far as the other side of London, in fact I was on the A1 thumbing a lift, and a Police Motorcyclist questioned me, I was, of course, in civilian clothes, I told him I was a soldier on weekend leave, unfortunately for me, he was an ex-military policeman. I was arrested and spent the night in Barnett Police station. The next morning I had to appear in the Magistrates court, handcuffed, and put in the back of police van and taken to the court, which was across the road! I was remanded in custody to await a military escort. Later that day two Welsh Guards arrived, again they handcuffed me, and used me as their personal battering ram on the London Underground.

I was taken to Scotland Yard, bet you didn't know, I certainly didn't, that the military have, or did have, a section there. Now remember this is the British Army and this me, I was under close arrest, (which means no trouser belt and no boot laces), so when I stood to attention my trousers fell down, lack of buttons coupled with a poor fit. Everything had to be done, 'on the double' which was marching up and down very fast, which resulted in my boots falling off, this was due to the Army's instruction, here fit this!

Even getting into a bath, was on the double, they gave me this tiny piece of soap, which I promptly lost, it went down the plug hole, another charge, losing Army kit, I remember being viewed as a bit of an oddity because I didn't smoke. I came to this conclusion because they didn't know how to handle me, in so much as all bribes and rewards were centred around cigarettes, a non smoker was something they hadn't encountered before.

I was there a couple of days before my Unit came to collect me, no handcuffs this time, just put in the back of a Landover with a guard. The other time I did a bunk, I travelled by train, first to Euston Station, and let me say that I can understand what they mean about panicking, every time you saw either a Policeman or an Army Redcap (Military Police), you imagine that they are looking for you, but then hey presto I'm home, well nearly, Stoke Station, as I was walking along Leek Road in the direction of Bucknall in the early hours of the morning, when I was stopped by the Police, when questioned I told them that my Mother was ill and I'd applied for compassionate leave which had been refused, the policeman took me home, and said "Look lad just remember all coppers aren't bastards, as long as you promise me that as soon as you've seen your mum and satisfied yourself that she's o.k. you will return to your unit later to-day." I thanked him very much, praying he wasn't going to wait till my Mum came to the door, as she was at work at Bucknall Hospital!

Well I think it was two or three weeks or even longer, before I decided to go back to Aldershot, this was because after a period of say three weeks AWOL you became a deserter, which was big trouble, I wasn't daft enough to put myself into that league, anyway it so happened that there was a special offer on the trains to London, so there I was on a Saturday morning at Stoke Station, I hadn't realized that the reason for the cheap train fare was that Manchester United was playing in the cup final at Wembley.

The result, I appeared amongst the crowds of Football supporters on the front page of The Evening Sentinel, I hoped that the nice policeman didn't see it. So it was back to the Guardroom, I remember reporting to the guards, asking politely is that 23246711 Stanton's name up on the board as AWOL, obviously the answer was a resounding yes! and the look on their faces when again in an equally polite voice, telling them to take it down, as I was here! So here I was back in the clink, and back to being a Church of Scotland attendee.

This was the period when the Comet Aeroplanes, had been grounded, our barracks, Malta Barracks, was situated next door to Laffans Plain, well that's how it is referred to on a map, it is in fact Farnborough Airfield, apparently some body from our outfit had breached security and stolen some instruments from the aircraft, know I knew nothing about this, but the

Sergeant Major claimed I must have been involved in it, as I was involved in all the mischief in the camp. What happened to the lads I never found out, I know the police were involved, and that the Sergeant Major was disappointed!

It was shortly after this that I had to attend another Medical Board, to discuss my "illness" this time when the question came "Do you like the Army" I was ready for it, I broke down in tears saying " I loved it, it was my chosen career etc" they responded with, "Well Son you are behind in your studies" etc, they were very sorry but I was considered Medically Unfit however because they could see what a profound effect it had on me, in 18 month's time I could apply for the men's army".

As I walked out on a cloud of happiness my friend the Sergeant Major was passing he looked at me and made some comment, oh the joy to smile and ignore him, I'd have given him a V sign if I'd dared to!

Job 7 Co-op Milk, Sneyd Green, Assistant Milkman

Fresh out of the army found me working at the Co-op Dairies, which has long since been demolished, although where it once stood, is a housing estate called Dairyfields. As I didn't have a regular round I covered the holiday rotas. My memory is a little scant however, I can remember a couple of the rounds, one was the Cheadle area, the driver was an ex-

Korean veteran I think his name was Roy. I remember he had a couple of fingers missing due to his action in the war; he was amused by my army story of "Working my Ticket" Another run I covered was Bradwell, the driver, sorry Milkman, was a bit of a lad for the ladies, he would give me the calls say on the left hand side of a road, whilst he did the right, this particular day I did my side, got back, no mate, I waited and waited, about 30 minutes later he strolled up, all smiles claiming in his words "I had to give Mrs so and so, one over the washing machine", I was amused especially when he exclaimed "It's all part of the job lad."

I remember two other drivers, one I liked working with, called Webby, he was a character, the vehicles were Electric Floats, well that's if you were on local runs, we were coming down Newcastle Street, Burslem, he knocked it out of drive so that it would freewheel and get some real speed up. Unfortunately it went that fast the half shafts sheered off, there were bits of metal all over the road, and he's there shouting to anyone in hearing distance "Beware a Sputnik has landed."

The other driver I can recall was a big fellow named Greg, what I couldn't stand about him was though he was always very smartly dressed, apparently he had recently got married, and he was for ever telling you and others about his sex life, I thought then and still do, married life is private and not up for discussion.

Job 8. Hanley Motor Cycles, Broad Street, Hanley. Trainee Motor Cycle Mechanic

However not for long, although this was my fault, I was young and stupid; I was sacked for joy riding at night in the firms van! Well VW pickup truck, remember I couldn't even drive, well not legally. The shop was where the Potteries museum is now, and I was the proud owner of a BSA Bantam 125cc motor bike, very noisy but fun, they claimed BSA stood for "Bloody Sore Arse" in reality it stood for, Birmingham Small Arms.

I was test driving a little moped one day, can't remember the make, but as I approached Howard Place, Shelton, a double decker bus was pulling away from the stop, I reduced speed, then opened up the throttle and slipped the clutch. I had forgot it was pre select, it reared up and I was running down the road with it, with only the back wheels making contact with road, no damage, only to my pride.

Another time a red three wheel Isetta bubble car was delivered, it was on the back of a transit type pick up truck, because it was a three wheeled vehicle, three planks were required, anyway as it was being carefully manoeuvred down the planks, only the front two wheels were visible you couldn't see the single rear wheel, someone over steered, no it wasn't me, off the car tumbled, bounced a couple of times, landed the right way up, and was soon made as good as new!

Then there was the time a customer came in and wanted to trade his motor bike and sidecar in, he wanted a straight swap for a smaller bike, the shop wasn't interested in the deal, my ears picked up, I asked him for his address, which was Meir Square, his bike was an Aerial square four, a big powerful bike, anyway, he was interested, lucky I insisted on a test ride, I couldn't steer the damn thing, because of the camber of the road, and probably the weakness in my arms, so it was a no go.

Incidentally the guy who owned the Motorcycle shop was Graham Bourne, who went on to form Bourne Leisure, the holiday camp giants. We had a part time Saturday salesman, Don McGraff, his full time occupation was a fitter at Meaford Power Station, he went on to start a very successful self drive business called VH, and sold out to Cowies becoming a millionaire.

Job 9. Castle Hotel Ironmarket, Newcastle. Hall Porter, Lounge Waiter

The job description says it all, not a bad job as it had its fiddles, bear in mind Newcastle Town Centre was a different layout then, the A34 came straight through the town centre, so the hotel had a lot of passing trade. I loved the orders, tea for three or four, as the ticket to the kitchen would be for two, and I'd slip the extra cups on and pocket the difference.

Friday and Saturday nights were always busy as the hotel had its own ballroom and a resident band, you had the regulars, hooray henrys, I called them. To impress their girl friends they would call out "I say William can I have a light ale?" etc., my response would be "Certainly, would Sir like a Double Diamond?," the answer was always "yes" they never got one, they had a Watneys Pale Ale, it was cheaper, well to me, not to them!

Next door to the Hotel was a departmental store called Pauldens, they had their Christmas dinner dance at the hotel, I was doing something on the stage when one of spotlights fell over and hit me on the head, accident unit that night, nothing other than a bump.

It was from Pauldens where I met a young lady from Chesterton, she was a member of the Salvation Army, I had been to their house one day on my motor bike, when a child ran out from behind an ice cream van, fortunately, I was not travelling at speed, however, contact was unavoidable, but I came off the worse, suffering burns to my leg, off the hot

exhaust pipe. The child's mother thanked me saying "Thank God it was a bike, who could take evasive action, had it been a car, he would have suffered more serious injuries."
This friendship was short lived, as her parents had a religious future planned for her, that didn't include me, I mean could you see me playing the tambourine or the big drum!

The headwaiter Eric was a strange fellow, I didn't know this at the time but he was having an affair with one of the waitresses, she called it off, so he jumped to his death from the Hotel roof, this was after I'd left though.

Fast forward from 1958 to 2011, working on a Wardle contract, in conversation with the school escort, I asked her if she originated from Newcastle, "Yes" she said, "born and bred in Newcastle," I asked her if she could remember the Castle Hotel, she replied "Oh yes, my dad worked there, Maurice" I said to her "You didn't come from Newcastle, you lived at Marina Drive, May Bank," how on earth did I remember that, well as I said, "Yes I can remember that, but not what I had for tea last night".

Job 10 Michelin Tyre Company Stoke. Tyre Worker
The trouble with this job, was twofold, one I got myself injured and two it was three shifts, Days, Noon's and Nights. Days was alright six – two, you did have time for a social life, noon's

was a no brainer two till ten, by the time you had clocked off, and made your way off the factory it would be about 10.15 p.m., in those days, last orders in pubs was 10.20p.m. closing time 10.30 p.m. and out of the premises by 10.40 p.m. Night shift was alright except when it came to week ends you finished work at 6 am Saturday morning, you went to bed, had a sleep because you were tired, then you couldn't sleep Saturday night etc, then it was 6 am Monday start, I'll tell you my bowels didn't like it!,

I worked in Department RX which was the Trindle shop, this was working with the wire reinforcing in the tyre walls, it came in coils about 10 inches in diameter, well one day a full one hit my right big toe, causing a fracture, and I've never managed to grow a toe nail since. After a period off sick I was put on light work, I did a week in another department, Rubber Mixing, it smelt and was heavy dusty work, so good bye Michelin.

I had bought myself a little moped to cope with the shift patterns, an NSU Quickly, in line with the explanation of what BSA stood for, NSU was nicknamed No Sodding Use, although to be fair I didn't have many problems with mine, however, I can recall one morning coming home after a night shift, along Leek Road, just past Bottleslow Street, it had been snowing, and coming towards me was a Beckets single deck bus, as it passed me, it caused a tidal wave of slush to engulf me, as this hit me, the chain on the moped snapped, this meant a two mile walk pushing the dam thing!

Job 11 Potteries Motor Traction. Bus Conductor

Now this was a job that most of the time I enjoyed, I say most of the time because I still had trouble controlling my temper, and dealing with the public could be stressful, but being honest I was too quick with my fists, and going back to my army days, same trouble, I didn't like discipline, but the drivers and conductors were a great bunch of blokes, and I'm still friends with some to this day.

The depot superintendent Bob Fox and I didn't get on, he had a reputation for begging cigarettes in return for giving employees plus rota (overtime) well I didn't smoke and didn't want extra hours, so I would taunt him with comments about his reputation, plus he was easy to wind up, like the time I had done something wrong and had been to Head Office on a disciplinary, for which I was suspended for two days, Bob hit the roof when I told him, that I had been awarded the two days and I'd have them off Saturday and Sunday!

I approached him one day and enquired about a transfer to Fenton Garage, this procedure if granted, normally took four to six weeks, I was granted it straight away and started at Fenton the following day. The reason for the request to transfer was

I'd recently been banned from driving for two years, and it was easier for get staff buses to Fenton. After I'd done half of the driving ban, I appealed claiming undue hardship, shift patterns etc, which I won, passing my driving test (this was the reason I'd been banned, three offences of driving un-supervised and without L plates) the day before my 21st birthday, so on June 27th 1961, I became legally entitled to drive.

A couple of characters worth mentioning, one a driver, most defiantly queer (you call them Gay's we called them Queers) who called himself Gorgeous George, his favourite trick with new conductors was at the start of the shift, without any warning, turn and face you, with a vivid coloured lipstick on, asking your opinion if the colour suited him. The other, was a conductress named Irene, not young, she could tell some amusing stories especially when she had been drinking the one I recall was; "it was late and she decided to get a taxi home, to Etruria Vale, she waited at the Taxi rank, one pulled up, she got in, a drunk also got in, as he got in he put his hand on her knee, she looked at him, and said, "Tits first," he immediately got out!"

It was working on this job that gave me my aversion to sugar in coffee and tea, the staff canteen was staffed by a couple of ladies, one of whom had suffered injuries to her hand whilst working at the Swynerton Munitions factory during the war; by injuries I mean that on one hand she had no fingers only stumps.

The canteen was very busy especially with hot drinks, so the serving hatch had all the mugs placed on one side, ready with the milk in them, say you asked for a tea, with sugar, she would slide the mugs across to the sugar container, to do this she would put the stumps of her fingers into the mug, however if you didn't take sugar you helped yourself, don't get me wrong she was a lovely lady, who couldn't help her disabilities, but the sight of her stumps in my mug used to go through me! So it was "No Sugar thank you"

It was about this time that buses were being introduced with doors on, until then they had been open platforms, these were both front and rear loaders.

 At Hanley Garage there was myself and Les Bolderson who were the young ones, and we both lived up to the banter, quickly earning ourselves nicknames, Les's was Knicker Ripper Bolderston, whilst mine was Scrape Arse Stanton, allow me to explain that these names only related to how quickly we rang the bell for the driver to proceed.

Again at Hanley, there was an acute shortage of buses, so until replacement ones could be bought in, buses were hired in, the ones I can recall were ex- Stratford Blues, Old Half Cab single Deckers, with a capacity of about thirty five, actually they were a waste of time, don't forget in those days, buses were very busy, after two stops on the Blurton number 46 route, the bus was full. Anyway my tale is about the day we were on duplicates, running from Hanley to Burslem, as we pulled up to the queue in Hanley, the driver slid his cab window back and shouted out "Burslem", bear in mind PMT buses were red, with destination blinds, we were in a strange blue bus, anyway, as I've said the driver as he slowly drew pass the queue shouted Burslem, someone shouted back "Turn left its about two miles down the road"

Job 12 Emanuel Bros. Ice Cream Salesman

I've got my driving licence know, and with that the worlds your oyster. I did actually start as an Ice Cream van salesman, it was for Mr Softy from Biddulph, but my stay was a very short one, this was because on my first day out on my own, I ate so much ice cream, it lowered my body temperature. It started in the night, fortunately my Mother was not working that night, so she soon had things under control, like blankets and hot drinks, my body was in uncontrollable spasms, I do believe the medical term is a Rigor.

The vehicle I was driving was a Commer Purpose Built Soft Service Van, in fact there is still one of these vans operating in the city as I write, it is parked in Hanley City Centre, by the Shopping Centre, owned and operated by Lewis's Ice Cream, Birches Head, its in immaculate condition and must be over fifty years old!

Job 13 Hancock Engineers & Fabricators. Van Driver

Driving a pick up truck for Hancock Engineering, this was a firm of fabricators who specialized in the Food industry, mainly Abattoirs; it involved some pretty smelly work. The two incidents I can recall were both on the same job at Tipton near Wolverhampton; it was at Hipkins the well known sausage manufacturers. The first one was driving back late at night and the fog had dropped making visibility very poor, both front and rear, I was carrying a long piece of metal tube which protruded from the vehicle a considerable length, so I made my way to Wolverhampton Police Station asking if I could leave the tubing there, the police were very obliging and agreed with my request, I asked for directions back to the A34, the Police gave me directions, pointing out that it was no problem just as you leave the Police station the street is one way, yes you've guessed it, I'd just drove down this street, in the wrong direction!

The other incident was again driving back late at night from a job, along the A34 in between Gailey Roundabout and Penkridge, it was pitch black and it had been a long day so I was half asleep, when all of a sudden there was this enormous noise along side me, it was a steam train travelling at about sixty mph. That woke me up!

Job 14. Clover Dairies Wellesley Street, Shelton. Milk Man

The site is now Student accommodation, I covered the Chesterton area. I thought I was in big trouble one day; the job was basic pay plus all kinds of bonuses, such as the numbers of empty bottles you bought in, sale targets, debts were deductible, even breakages were taken into account, well on this occasion I had lost a call, a good call, about four pints daily. I enquired at the house and the woman explained that it was nothing that I had done, but a relation of hers had started work for a rival company and she'd given him the business to help him get started, later that day I happened to bump in to him, words were exchanged and he ended up with a black eye.

When I got back to the depot I was called into the managers office, for what I thought would be the sack, with the manager was another male who it transpired was the proprietor of the rival company, he was dancing up and down saying things like, "I was a thug", and "why didn't I try to punch him?" when I agreed to his request to go outside, thinking well I've nothing to lose, I've got the sack, he calmed down and was satisfied that I would be dealt with within Clover Dairies guide lines, without the need to do anything else. I was told to cash up and come back to the office afterwards, which I did, only to met with a smile and a handshake saying it was a pity more of the staff were so keen on their job!

The trouble with this job, was the vehicle, a three wheel milk float, when you left the depot in the morning, fully charged up, it wasn't too bad, but as the day went on it got slower and slower and sometimes you practically crawled back to the depot, and you try and steer a three wheeler through snow, believe me you followed the troughs, no cab doors, no heaters.

Occasionally one of my customer's daughters who was also employed by Clover, and if it was her day off, would make me a cup of tea, and then come and give me a hand. On this particular occasion we were in Heath Street, Chesterton she had gone to this house and was chatting away to the customer, she shouted to me to come and join them, I went up to the house and joined in this most strange conversation, my helpmate was listening to this tale about the woman's husband trying to poison her and the cat, my mate was goading her saying she knew him, and that she had the same surname, Scott.

At this the woman said, "Tell you what all three of us, as Roman Catholics, will go down to the court balcony to watch and throw stones at him, whilst he was being crucified," I couldn't get out of the house quick enough, I found out later that she suffered from schizophrenia, years later when I worked on Beresford Buses I often used to see her periodically in the grounds of Cheddleton Hospital, although I never spoke to her.

Job 15 Staffordshire Farmers. Lorry Driver

My first job lorry driving, I applied for the job, and was given a driving test, that went alright until it came to reversing the damn thing, either they were desperate for drivers or the poor guy in the passenger seat felt sorry for me, I got the job!,

It was hard work just driving the lorry, it was an ancient Guy Vixen, and its gear box was behind you, just driving it, up and down the gearbox made your shoulder ache! One day I'd been working in the fields, by what is now the Douglas McMillan Hospice; the lorry had been loaded, when I say loaded, it was done by hand, my hands! with sacks of Barley, as I came to the cross roads, again as it was then, very slowly, double clutch, change down from third, into second then into first, clutch out slowly, oops it was in reverse!

It was hard physical work, but the load I always struggled with, was bales of hay, they weighed about a hundred weight (cwt), but the bulk of it was the killer. Another notorious heavy weight that had to be collected from Whey Products in Haslington near to Crewe, were small drums of cattle food weighing 2cwt, one of its ingredients was lead pellets!

Linda used to come with me at times, her job was to open and close the farm yard gates. One particular time, my brother Tommy was on leave from the Navy and he came with me for a day out, the farm I was delivering to, was situated somewhere near to Moorville Hall, and involved a reversing manoeuvre. Tommy was out of the cab watching me backup, shouting "come on, come on", Bang, I could see the wall of the Barn vibrating, then I heard Tommy shout Wow! Too late.

Another time, again Tommy was with me, and again it involved reversing, I was leaning out of the cab with the cab door open, when I fell out, Tommy looked round, there was me climbing back into cab, the tick over had prevented the engine from stalling.

Job 16. Whitehurst Builders of Trent Vale, Tipper Driver
When I went for the interview, it sounded a great job, picking up loads of sand & gravel and delivering to various building sites around the area. First day that's what I did, loaded up at

the Gravel Pits and tipped at the site, I thought ay up kid, this is a good life, then came the shock, for the rest of the time I was there, which was another week, it was loading and delivering best bricks which meant they had to handballed on and off, after a week of this, even holding a newspaper would make my fingers bleed! I thought there's got to be an easier way to earn a living! So it was on yer bike Billy Boy!

The site I delivered these bricks is at Heron Cross, it was for a purpose built dining hall, at a school. I recently picked up a child from this school for Wardle's, it certainly stirred a memory or two.

Job 17 Co-op Bakery Newport Lane, Middleport. Bread Man (Coincidentally my mate Mario has these same premises now).
My first round covered the areas of Endon, Bagnall, Werrington, Caverswall and Meir, the custom of tipping at Christmas was prevalent both in money, gifts and alcohol. All bread, cakes & biscuits had to be pre-ordered, well the long and short of it, yours truly was drunk, (No breathalyzer in those days) at the end of the run which was about 11.00 p.m. Christmas Eve, I didn't have the correct stock left, apparently I left Malt Bread for Small Hovis loaves!

I hadn't been there long when it transferred to a new purpose built bakery which had been built at Knutton; the site is now Morrison's. At Middleport we were known as the Burslem Co-Operative Society, we were now part of the North Midlands Co-Op, which for us was a plus and minus situation, the plus was that a lot of money was been invested in updating the fleet, the minus was that we lost the supply of freshly made confectionary, and had to sell pre packed Red Rose cakes, this may seem a minor issue but the trouble and truth of the matter was that Co-Op bread was not a good product to sell, even with the new bakery in production.

With this merger came new areas, I was given the Rugeley area, I would be there at six in the morning. The bread was hot to the touch, but by the time I had got to Rugeley the bread was drying up, in the past you had the confectionary to fall back on, so it was a struggle to hit targets.

As I've stated new vehicles were constantly being delivered and because my round was considered distance, and ideal for running them in, I had a supply of new vans to drive, well I was, until I was done for speeding. I had even gained some good new calls including a Monastery at Abbots Bromley, (Hawk's Yard) but to be caught speeding in a new van, now that was a cardinal sin. Shortly after this I was back on the local areas, but not before this tale, we had a system that any fresh confectionary left on the van on a Saturday night was disposed of, I used to make sure there was sufficient left over for my own consumption.

The confectionary was kept in a purpose built side locker in the van body, I had unloaded all my bread returns, went to the side locker knowing what was in there, lo and behold it was empty, not even any trays. Well I thought this is a wind up, so I played up to it, accusing everyone, no one admitted to it, so I made my way to the supervisors office, no one in, so I made further enquires as to where he was, and was told that he been called out to the Rugeley area; one of the vans had gone round a bend that fast he'd lost all his trays of confectionary and they were in someone's front garden! I never did hear the last of that one.

Still in Rugeley, I decided to introduce the residents to the pleasures of Oatcakes. Rugeley is in Staffordshire and they are a North Staffordshire delicacy, I explained the delights of having them warm and filled with bacon, cheese, sausages and tomatoes, or even as I liked them, with jam. After all this sales blurb I had secured orders for 20 dozen, great, the following week I came back with more than I had started with!

Anyway I am now back local, Bucknall, Werrington and Cheadle was my area. The winter of 1962/63 was a tough one, I often used to come home in the van, Linda's spent her fair share of time and effort pushing them, they were diesels and diesel wasn't as refined as it is now. This resulted in them constantly freezing up, even slush from the roads would result in the pipes freezing, so if you could manage to push it and get it rolling you would manage to pull the fuel through, I'm not talking here of little 5 cwt vans, these were vans with a gross carrying capacity of three tons, as Linda would testify.

It was the beginning of 1963, and it started snowing, I was in Cheadle when it started coming down, and boy oh boy did it come down, I abandoned the run about two o'clock and it was eleven at night when I got back to Knutton.

Job 18 Beresfords, Cheddleton Bus Conductor

This time with Beresford Buses back working as a conductor, I was a spare, in other words I didn't have my own regular route and covered sickness, holidays etc., I hadn't been there long and was doing the service 16 route Hanley–Leek, when I decided to go and see Jim Beresford and asked him for a cash bag, he looked at me and said "Who are you?" I told him, and explained that I was covering route 16, he looked back at me as if I was an idiot saying "What's up lad haven't you got pockets in that jacket." I thought to myself, if I'm using my pockets, some of the money will stay in it and it did.

I decided to buy myself a new NSU Quickly, a moped, from Halfords in Leek, so how do I get it back from Leek? I know what I'll do, at Leek Bus Station, I'll collect all the fares, and travel behind the bus to Cheddleton. I explained to the passengers when they wanted to get off, ring the bell the driver will stop I'll be riding behind, jump on the bus ring the bell to go, then jump off, similarly any passengers wishing to board the bus before Cheddleton, I would collect the fare before they got on the bus, it worked a treat, and caused much hilarity with the passengers, well it wasn't every day you see a bus conductor riding a Moped with a ticket machine round his neck, chasing after a bus.

Another incident that comes to mind, same route, another day, Jim Beresford called me into the office for a rollicking, I thought what is he on about, apparently I had allowed a woman in a Red Cross uniform to board the bus, "Yes" I said, "So what's wrong in that?" she had paid her fare same as everyone else, he went berserk ranting and raving about this woman travelling on his bus, it was his Mother!. My instructions was in future even if it meant telling the driver to drive past the stop leaving everyone behind, there was no way she was to travel on his buses.

Jim Beresford was one of those people who whilst close to brilliancy, was also close to lunacy, you've have heard the expression, the hair stood on end, well when he lost his temper, his hair used to literary stand up!

In between service runs we had to clean the buses, on this particular day I had cleaned out the double decker on my turn, and was making my way through the garage between the buses when Jim accused me of scratching the side of a coach, I denied it, so he grabbed the buckle of my overalls scratched the side of a coach and said, "That's how you did it"! And stormed off.

Beresford's at the Potters Holidays always made sure that the breakdown truck was serviced, because in those days Potters Holidays meant that half the fleet would be on holiday excursions, a memory that always brings a smile to my face was seeing a Beresfords Double Decker on the North Wales Express Service, all points from Rhyl to Llandudno, followed closely by a large furniture van. This was carrying the luggage, the thing that caught my eye, was the previous owners of the furniture van was proudly displayed all over the vehicle, Farley's Rusks.

One of the contracts they did, for the summer months only, was to go on hire to Smiths Tours of Wigan (which you now know as Shearings) touring the Isle of Wight, the driver would travel light to Wigan on a Sunday, collect the party and off to do a six day tour. He would return the following Friday. Saturday was his designated day off, then Sunday he would have to do it all again, anyhow on this Friday I had to meet him at Hanford, the driver was Jim Mountford, apparently Jim had rang in sick and was expecting a relief driver to take the coach onto Wigan.

At Hanford then there was a little café, these were the days before the M6 or even any other Motorways, there I was awaiting his arrival, the coach pulled up, he very gingerly climbed out of the cab, and made his way to me, I could tell he look puzzled as he knew I was a conductor, I handed him a parcel, he hit the roof calling Jimmy Beresford all the names he could think of, his sickness was piles and my parcel had contained a rubber ring for him to sit on! The poor bloke had to carry onto Wigan, more about Beresford's later.

Job 19 Blackpool Corporation Bus Conductor/Trams Job 20 Bus Driving

I went for an interview about gaining employment there, I was successful, subject to me having a Blackpool address, so I managed to get lodgings at an elderly ladies house (Mrs Joy) in Duke Street, which was just around the corner from the depot. After a few days living there I enquired if it was alright to have a bath, she replied that it wouldn't be a problem, but I would have to give her a hand. I was a bit mystified as to what she meant by giving her a hand, my bedroom was the bathroom! The bath had a mattress that fitted over it to make a bed, I don't recall her ever taking a bath.

Before I start telling you about this job, this would have been late 1964, I must tell you about the time I hired a van to collect a studio couch my Mother had given us. I'd hired this van and these were the days when heaters in vehicles were extras so there were none fitted. We had had the weekend in Stoke and were returning on Sunday night, we set off leaving Stoke about 9 pm, when the fog dropped, I say fog it was in fact smog! To join the M6 you had to travel to Arclid, Junction 17, as the M6 had not been completed, and then it only went as far as Preston, it took us nine hours to get to Blackpool, it was a journey from hell, Linda was asleep in the back on the studio coach, my Mother was in the front with me. It was freezing fog, you couldn't see more than a yard in front of you, at one time I had a pee in a bottle in an attempt to clear the ice off the screen but that only made it worse. When I say Linda was asleep, this was in fact due to her feeling unwell, she was pregnant with Tracy, but didn't know it at the time!

I started there as a bus/tram conductor, and the job offer was for the summer season, my staff number being 5089, at the end of the season I was offered fulltime employment and my

staff number changed to twenty nine this offer suited me, as
on the 21st October 1963 Linda and I, the sweetheart I had left
behind, got married.

Shortly after this the Transport & General Workers Union
organised a night out in Blackburn, it was the social clubs
football club, if you wanted to go you just put your names
down ,which I did, but then as Linda was not that keen, I
cancelled. They hired a self-drive minibus for the occasion, the
designated driver I can only remember his name as Geordie,
on the return journey the minibus crashed and two were killed.
Geordie was sent to prison for drink driving; on his release he
told us some pretty horrendous stories of life behind bars, in
fact to horrendous to put into print, I should explain that the
incidents were not related to him.

The work system at Blackpool was very different than Stoke,
at Stoke you had a different driver each week as per your rota;
at Blackpool you had your own regular partner, mine being
Bob Alison, who was about six foot five of muscle, he claimed
to be French Canadian, and had served in the Canadian
Royal Air force, but was also a queer, even though he was
married with a wife and children. At meal break time instead
of, as all the others did at Talbot Road Bus Station, which was
eat and relax in the canteen; he would in his words, nip round

to the Library/Art Gallery and help his mate adjust some pictures!

I bought a second hand tape recorder from him, to be fair, he did say don't listen to what was already on the tape, but that only increased my curiosity, he had recorded himself, or some one else, urinating into what sounded like a toilet bowl! At times his driving was erratic and could be quite frightening, especially if some one else was at fault, like the time a van failed to stop at a crossroads, Bob made no effort at stopping and hit the van side on, forcing it on to its side, names and addresses were exchanged, and as I've said because of his build, he looked very intimidating. The van driver showed me the business card Bob had given him, it read, Flight Lieutenant R Alison, private tuition in civil aviation, and the phone was his staff number!.
Bob told me a story that when he was in the Air Force whilst travelling through India by train he had been raped! Several times and ended up in hospital, how true this was I'll never know, he was after all a Walter Mitty character!

When I was offered the chance to do Driver Training, I jumped at the opportunity, well I was after all an experienced lorry driver, or so I thought. The driving instructor went through my past driving experiences with me, and then took me out of the depot (Manchester Square) left into Lytham Road, left into

Bloomfield Road, when I felt my pants going warm! I was in a front wheel skid! The instructor smiled, a kind of smile that says he was expecting this. What I hadn't realised was that the bus, which was an ancient open top double decker, had a narrow wheel base, it was seven foot six inches wide instead of eight foot two inches which was the norm, his comments were "Thought you could drive did you?"

I soon got to master the beast, no synchronised gearbox, heavy duty clutch pedal, no sound proofing. The engine was there with you in the cab, to turn the steering wheel at times, you had to stand up! Perhaps now Keith, my son, will understand why I can't get excited by these vintage buses, we had to drive the damn things for twelve hours a day!

The fleet at Blackpool consisted of only one type of vehicle, Double Deckers, at the time I passed my test there was only two models, although new PD3's were joining the fleet, all were Leyland's, there was PD1's & PD2's. The PD1's were centre door staircase, whilst the PD2's and the PD3's were rear platforms. When the PD3's arrived, they were the first half cabs to join the fleet, prior to this they were double fronted. This meant you shared your cab with the engine at all times, fine in winter but not so good in summer, the centre door type had a tendency to loose the backend on a wet surface, which was quite alarming to the travelling public, especially when they could see the driver turning round and grinning.

Even though new drivers had passed the test, they had to demonstrate there capability of driving all three models, pulling away, changing down, yes, through all the gears, even into first, plus reversing. I had no problem until I got into this brand new PD3 direct from Leyland, it was at first a joy to drive, until it came to changing down, I got it stuck in first gear, it had to go back to Leyland like this, I was comforted to know that it was a fault not caused by me.

Before I go onto driving let me tell you about the day I was conducting on a very busy route, and a passenger pointed out to me that someone had left a large cardboard box under the stairs, my eyes lit up, as the lost property rules were, all perishable good's could be claimed at the end of your shift, whilst other goods were retained for three months. If the goods were not claimed they were returned to you, but if they were claimed you received ten per cent of the value. So come to the end of shift and it's still there, tied up with string; I gently opened it, it was full of bird/chicken droppings!

Even though I was now a fully qualified PSV driver there was this antiquated system, that was based on seniority, say I was down to drive and the conductor missed their turn, the spare conductor may have been a driver working his rest day, and if he had been employed there longer than me, he could claim the turn and I'd have to conduct.

I also drove the trams a few times, but as least as possible, they were uncomfortable things, sitting on a shelf for eight plus hours a day. In an emergency, stopping was controlled by your hand switching the control to zero power, whilst your heel was used to operate a floor mounted switch that released sand onto the track this was because it was metal on metal. It wasn't for me I left the tram driving alone if I could. To drive them, no licence was required only a police test. Fortunately for me there was a surplus of tram drivers, as two depots had had their routes closed, one depot was Bispham and other one was Whitegate Drive.

Once you took the tram out, you were stuck with it, no nipping out to the shop etc, we used to carry Billy Cans, with a supply of tea, (tea bags hadn't been invented) milk and sugar, and at designated points there were brewing facilities. One day as we approached the pleasure beach, one tram ran into back of the tram in front, the driver of the offending tram was covered in tea leaves, although he strenuously denied that he had been drinking tea. If there was any kind of problem on the track, it soon backed up, for you could only pass in limited passing

places, so if the tram in front had a crew that was either new
or slow, you had it quiet and they had it busy.

On the buses the banter between the drivers, well the young
ones, was if you couldn't go along the prom at 50 mph, with
your hand on the horn, on a Bank Holiday Monday you were a
failure! I'd qualified, and by now I had my own regular mate,
Christine, she was eighteen the same age as Linda, and was
scooter mad. One day she gave me a lift home, well, we were
weaving in and out of traffic and when she dropped me off,
she smiled and said "How was that?" I replied "Christine you
frightened me that much you've bought me on a week early!"
the following day she said, "Bill I didn't know men had
periods," she was that innocent.

The job/wages was great in the summer season, but in winter
that would change as there was a vast labour surplus and
hours were scarce. I also had a problem with a re-occurring
back problem, when I was nineteen I had been involved in a
head-on car crash, one day it went whilst I was driving and the
ambulance crew had to get me out of the cab. Linda wondered
what on earth was going on, she could hear a commotion and
men's voices coming up the stairs, there I was being gently
levered into our flat! That was nothing to the passengers
faces, especially those who'd been on the bus from the start of
the journey from South Pier, on the buses arrival at Talbot

Square, the ambulance men were waiting to get me out of the cab!

One of the routes I used to be regularly rotated on was the number 12, Talbot Road Bus Station to Squires Gate Airport, (now known as Blackpool Airport) it was a busy route and on this day I had a conductress named Audrey working with me, she had a bit of a reputation, but we won't go into that. I had one of the new Deckers a PD3, when we stopped at Manchester Square, she came round to me complaining about a youth, causing her trouble. I said "OK, if he causes any more trouble, you know the emergency system, ring four bells," as we approached Central Pier I was watching her in my interior mirror, as she put her hand up to the overhead strip bell, I counted one, two, three, and then four, as she pressed the bell for the fourth time, I stood on the brakes. The bus practically stood on end, but instead of her holding onto the seats, she came flying backwards down the bus, slamming against the bulkhead, he, the aggressor also came down the bus aisle like an arrow, colliding into her, she suffered, (I think) bruised ribs. I jumped out of the cab, remember in those days all buses were rear loaders, just as this bloke was getting off, I challenged him, with the comments, "Where do you think you're going pal, you'd better sit there until the police arrive," which he promptly did.

I ran down to the Central Pier area, where there was always a Police van parked up, complete with officers in the rear, ready for action, it was late at night, in no time the police had him in the back of the van, and believe me the Police in Blackpool don't mess about, especially with drunks! The following day he appeared in court, what happened to him I can't remember, but I can remember Audrey's comments, she felt sorry for him, as he was after all quite handsome except he had no front teeth! Whether he had teeth before clashing with the police, I don't know.

It may come as no surprise to you, but in the summer, and we are talking about the period 1963–1968 the buses were very busy, especially route 12 and 5, these were the ones that operated along the promenade. To alleviate the problem, conductors would be rotated to work as what was called "Jumpers", they would jump on your bus and collect the fares, say the conductor was collecting fares on the lower deck, then the jumper would collect the fares on the top deck. They would also stand at the bus stop and collect the fares, usually at the Tower or on the return Manchester Square. They would issue green tickets against our white ones, it was a system that worked well, I myself did several stints as a Jumper, particularly as a way of working your rest day (overtime).

However, what no one had realised was that a guy called Chris was doing this in his own time, he had obtained a stolen ticket machine from a competing company, Ribble Bus, and was making himself a small fortune, he only got found out, by his own greed. A passenger had complained to him, that he had short changed her, it was only coppers, but he refused a refund and the lady complained in writing, enclosing the ticket. The offices inspection revealed that the machine's number did not tally up with any of theirs, he got jailed for it, silly fellow if only he'd not been greedy!

During my time there as a driver I only ever had one accident, and that wasn't my fault. I was driving past Stanley Park, cars parked both sides of the road, a car was coming towards me, I thought if he doesn't give way, I won't get through, he didn't give way and I didn't get through, see what I mean? I was right wasn't I, anyway the cars driver, was jumping up and down saying he was going to call the Police, (no mobiles in those days); I said "Please yourself pal, but I'm going to get out of my cab, what do you want me to do, jump on to your roof or the bonnet," he moved, Result, no proof, no case to answer as who was to blame, knock for knock. However I did agree that it was my fault as long as the Police were not involved, otherwise I would have been done for driving without due care and attention.

We will finish off tales of Blackpool Buses by telling you about Linda, she had got herself her job at Lewis's Departmental Store, and asked me if it was alright to go to the annual Christmas Party, no problem, but it's staff only, no partner's, no problem. When the night came, as she came out of the Winter Gardens where the function had been held, there was a row of Blackpool Corporation buses to take them home, bet you can guess who was driving Linda's bus.

I've included this because its funny, Linda's workmate/friend from Lewis's, was getting married and we were both invited. My eldest, Tracy was a baby, I was working on the docks at Preston, Saturday was half day working, so I had dashed home, for a quick wash and change of clothes, put on my only suit, which had been dry cleaned for the occasion, only to find that the zip fly had broken, panic all round. Linda took charge telling me we hadn't got time to mess around, she would do a repair on it as I was driving to the venue, our mode of transport was a van, and we lived in Cleveleys.

The wedding was in Lytham Road Blackpool, we arrived with minutes to spare, as I got out of the van, I was aware, and so were many more, that in her rush, she had not only used a large nappy pin, complete with a blue end, but she also had managed to attached her orange coloured glove to my trouser fly area, well as you can imagine it caused a few laughs, especially with my comments of "Oh she must have gone.........."

After the reception, the young ones, yes, we were young once, went into Blackpool to play Ten Pin bowling, but not before we went home for Linda to carry out a better repair on the offending fly zip. But by this time the shops had shut, so it had to be make do with what she'd got, which was press studs, which in theory and in an upright position worked, but not for playing Ten Pin Bowling, every time I took up the position to bowl, Ping, and I was open to the elements, we certainly had a laugh that night.

Job 21 Dockside Transhipper; Job 22 Artic Driver; Job 23 Forklift Driver. Northern Ireland Trailers (NITS), Preston Docks

Northern Ireland Trailers Ltd, or abbreviated to NITS, I cold called there one day to see about driving vacancies, they asked me about my previous driving experience which I slightly exaggerated, "O.K." they said "come along on Saturday morning and we'll give you a driving test."

The driving test consisted of driving a Leyland Comet Artic around Preston; complete with a twenty foot trailer loaded with pipes. I thought thank goodness it's only a short trailer, because contrary to what I claimed I had never driven an Artic before. All went well and I could tell the Foreman sitting as passenger was impressed until we got back and I had to reverse it into a limited space, I didn't know then, but I certainly do now, that the shorter the trailer the more difficult it is to reverse it, anyway this guy said, "Look it's obvious you have no experience driving Articulated Lorries, but I like your enthusiasm, yes, you've got the job, you'll soon pick it up working on the Docks"

So I started as a transhipper working all nights at first, one of NITS main jobs was the handling of dead pigs from Ireland, it would come in from various locations around both North & Southern Ireland, they were wrapped in sacking and just lay there on the trailers, no refrigeration in those days. Our job as transhippers would be to re-distribute them on to the correct forwarding addresses, one man would be driving the forklift truck, another one would be hooking them up and the third one would be landing them and positioning them into the correct order for the driver's route.

Sometimes the securing rope around the pig carcasses would break and the carcass would drop in the dirt of the warehouse yard, no problem, you'd just get the hosepipe and hose it down, sometimes even hosing the maggots off!
There would be three teams of three men, all working in a confined space of the warehouse. And yes, I gained the

necessary Artic Driving experience required. I remember one night it had rained all night, it was bitterly cold, and I was completely knackered I had shunted vehicles all over the docks, so it was a relief to be going home in the comfort of my own vehicle.

I had to reverse out and thought I was driving an Artic, putting the wrong steering lock on, result a damaged front wing! It was shortly after this that I changed from nights to days, longer hours but more money, plus I was promoted to Chargehand, looking after an in-house ICI contract, more of this job later. Another amusing story of the time, we sometimes used to give each other lifts to and from work, well that's if you were from the Blackpool area, on this occasion I was driving. My car was a Triumph Herald, there were four of us in the car, as I was driving along the main road, the bonnet lifted up, tilting forward, this actually resulted in twisting the chassis and the car being an insurance total loss, anyway here we are, its six o'clock in the morning, how do we get to Preston? We achieved this by one of the passenger's, the thinnest, lying across the bonnet, holding on to the corner of the drivers door, whilst the passenger held him by his ankles.

As I've said I became competent in not only Artic driving but forklifts too, it was about this time that the law was changed relating to HGV driving, to obtain your Class One licence, all you had to was to produce your copies of your drivers log books, however I'd had this recent promotion so I didn't take this option up.

It was common knowledge at the time of the fiddles that Dockers got up to, you name it, we could get it, and I'm afraid I was no different. I got involved with a couple of guys from Blackpool, Harry & Larry, yes that's their real names, who had the contract to take the scrap cardboard away from the ICI contract, with the benefit of hindsight I was stupid, they introduced me and Linda, to for the want of a better phrase, to the 'Blackpool Stars' We went as their guests to see Tony Bennett, Count Basie, Jayne Mansfield, often meeting Jack Rothenstall the script writer from Coronation Street and London's Burning. Jack was a very quite unassuming bloke and was often in Harry's house, Jack at the time was single he would later marry Maureen Lipman, but you were aware that he was always following conversations.

As an example my daughter Tracy had just been born, Harry congratulated us and asked the birth weight, 8lb 1oz was our proud answer, this fact was featured in an episode of Coronation Street, no names just in general talk in the script, like so and so has just had a baby, didn't she do well for her first born 8lb 1oz.

Anyway the legal contract of the removal of the waste cardboard soon became illegal, I was in total control of the contract, which was to oversee the grading of the bobbins from various mills from all around the UK. The bobbins were actually aluminium so had a good scrap value, so yours truly was illegally sending out what looked like loads of scrap cardboard, but was actually bobbins, and as a good many before me has done, I got greedy and careless, and got caught.

In a way I was lucky, the day it happened I was actually off sick, and had gone to Blackburn taking Tracy with me, who was then a toddler. When we left in the morning it was a bright sunny day, however it had changed and I rang Linda to say don't worry about Tracy as I'd bought her a coat. Linda told me some blokes had called and asked if Tom was in, now even though my first name is Thomas no one ever called me by that name, so I thought, strange, and rang Harry who was relieved to hear from me.

He explained that the Police had followed the lorry and arrested Larry; he said if I kept his name out of it, he would make sure that if I was sent to prison, Linda would be financially cared for, plus all legal costs would be met, I agreed to this, went home and was subsequently arrested.

Harry was as good as his word, he provided me with a good solicitor who managed to get the charges made out to a lower level of crime, and I was fined Thirty Pound's on each offence. I was actually charged with two offences of 'Theft as a Servant'. Harry helped me with contacts to start up as a market trader, I was amazed at some of the things I found out, such as he had an Ocean Going Yacht, and it was skippered by a Police Inspector!

As the case was waiting to go to court I had a visit from the C.I.D. who were investigating a lorry load of Maggies soups that had gone missing from the docks, it was suggested that if I were to supply information leading to the thieves being apprehended, they would sanction the sum of £200.00 as a reward. I denied all knowledge, and smiled inwardly at his comments; "personally I don't believe there has ever been a load missing, it was an insurance scam," I thought for God's sake don't look in our cupboards!

As I've said, on the docks you could get any thing, cigarettes, alcohol, clothing, tyres, even footwear, if it was transported, it was available. Alcohol was off the Polish ships, you used to get Gordons Gin that was coloured green, one of the lads, Cyril, wanting some Vodka, (this was 100% proof and spelt Wodka), said he must try it first, they opened a bottle, he took a swig, and it took the skin off his top lip, Cyril said "It's good stuff, I'll have a case." Another thing that was widely available was Tea, it was unblended and came in Tea Chests, that strangely enough used to burst open, well, one of the kitchen gadgets that was the rage at the time, was tea dispensers, you kept the top part filled up with tea, pressed a button and it dispensed a correct measure of tea, into the waiting teapot. This tea as I've said was unblended, so some of it was like logs, we used to say be careful, if you get two logs in your mug and they met it would smash it, on occasions the tea coming out of the dispenser would come out like sand.

I remember on one occasion I bought that much Pork home, it broke the shelves in our Fridge, another time I had come home from a night shift, and took home the wrong haversack, the one I'd bought home belonged to the crane driver and contained dangerous drugs, the Police called at our house and exchanged them, Linda was in a advanced stage of pregnancy and the Policeman took a shine to her, knowing that I worked long hours, he started making a habit of calling unannounced, I soon put a stop to this, calling at the local police station threatening him.

To get to work you had to have a reliable car, I bought a VW Beatle, nice car in red, on this occasion after work I'd gone for a drink with the lads, in Preston. On the way home I fell asleep for a second, woke up, thought ah yes, turn right, however, I was not on the bend where I thought I was, the car shot up the embankment, tearing about fifty yards of hedging out, before landing upside down in the road. I quickly got out, and it was just as well as I wasn't smoking, I was covered in petrol, the petrol tank being located at the front had spilled out soaking my clothing, the car was taken to a local garage and I arrived home as a passenger in a tow truck!

I arranged a lift to work for the following day, but I had to borrow a bike to get home, an eighteen mile journey, no lights and a very sore backside! The car was as far as I was concerned a write off, and I only had third party insurance, which was illegal as the car was on finance. So keeping that to myself, I did manage to do a swop with a guy, who had an old VW Beatle which was left-hand drive, I remember his words well, he asked me if I'd driven a LHD before, I answered truthfully," No" his advice was, "No problem just remember if you want to overtake anything, sit well back"

So there I was driving very carefully through Kirkham, I was aware that there was a Ribble bus in front, so remembering the words of advice, sit back, I did, and a Scooter ran in the back of me! These old Beatle cars, didn't have fuel gauges, you had a foot operated switch, I say switch, it was a piece of metal that you pushed over, switching over from the petrol tank to the reserve tank, you then had enough petrol for about another thirty miles, however on this one, the main tank had a slight leak.

One day Linda and I were out in it, driving through Preston towards Bamber Bridge, and came to road works, they were actually resurfacing the road, and were burning off the top surface, I quickly switched over to the reserve tank, luckily it was downhill, so we free wheeled, as we drove past with the flames seemingly touching the car, rest assured we both said our prayers!

TWS Supplies, High Street Kirkham Job 24 Shop keeper, Job 25 Market Trader

I became a carpet shop proprietor using my initials TWS; it was in the High Street Kirkham. I sold carpet remnants direct from the Mills. I bought it by weight; this was an introduction from Harry (previously mentioned). My main customers were prison officers from the nearby Kirkham Prison, one or two of them thought that they were clever in obtaining the goods and not paying for them, what they didn't realise was that I had some good contacts and a phone call to the Governor always did the trick. I even sold and fitted out a boutique in Preston and a Car Sales Office with carpet remnants, yes, I fitted them!

I bought a large Fordson van, stocked it out with carpets, lino, rugs and fancy goods, employed a man on commission only, and sent him to call on farmers, he also did a couple of markets for me, one in particular comes to mind, Casanew Street, in Liverpool, which is no longer there, in fact where the market was, is one of the entrances to the Mersey tunnel.

This was a market like no other, it would be the mid-sixties. Once I was very surprised to see a battery accumulator on sale, I'll bet ninety per cent of people don't know what one of those is, also on sale were even second hand nails, mugs without handles, used clothing etc. One thing that always amused me was the wallpaper vans, there were three different vans selling the wallpaper, we used to say the sweepings up!, this could be anything from the end of the rolls showing the red warning lines, to odd colours, even rolls that were torn. People were hanging onto the sides of the vans to get a bargain, it was sold for mere pennies, and they would sell out in record time. It was the kind of market that only sold rubbish; in fact you had to have three persons to man the stall, one to sell and the other two to guard your stock.

I also covered Chorley, Blackburn, Barrow in Furness, Ulverston and even Sandbach. I had changed to selling discounted wallpaper, to buy it in, was less fifty per cent, plus there was no purchase tax. What's purchase tax I hear you say? Well this was before VAT and was set at eleven per cent on top of the purchase price, same thing different name.

The thing was you didn't tell the customers that there wasn't any more available rolls, so if a customer was to say "I'll take those five rolls, but I may need another one" no problem you would assure them; then vanish for a few weeks.

Sandbach in the sixty's was a thriving half day market, the guy on the next stall to me was captivated by the claims of another stallholder who was selling ladder-proof ladies stockings, to demonstrate this he would run a nail file up the stocking. I think the retail price of these were in the region of one pound fifty, or as it was then, thirty bob, and he was selling them at ten bob, or fifty pence. This guy said that he was going to buy two pairs, one for the wife, and the other pair for the girl friend! I said to him something along the line that he must be crazy, as he knew that we only sold rubbish, but he was dead impressed by the demo, the following week he's ranting and raving, and stating what he was going to do to the seller, although I did wonder how he knew he hadn't got a father. I said "There you are, I told you they would ladder," he replied, "They didn't ladder, there was no feet in them!" and do you know we never saw the seller again!

I still remember my spiel selling the wallpaper; "At these prices you can do your front passage or your back passage, or any passage you want" it's amazing what a bit of banter would get you. Coming up to Christmas I would sell Christmas wrapping paper and had a line in Perfume, they were boxed in a very nice square box with some exotic name and the price of five guineas boldly displayed, all in Gold writing. In fact the boxes cost more than the perfume, I think it cost about two shillings, (ten pence) to buy and I used to sell it at five shillings, (twenty five pence). To get this price you would shout and display the product, invite the crowd to smell it, and then start off with the spiel, "I don't want five guineas, four, three or even two guineas, who'll give me a pound," you'd always get a couple of hands up, then you'd say, "If ten of you raise yours hands up I'll knock it down to ten bob" (fifty pence) and keep reducing till you were at your selling price.

By this time you would have a sizable numbers of punters, of course you would entertain them with comments like "it contains the new wonder ingredient, 'SH one T', as you may have guessed the perfume that was opened for their invitation to sample and smell was not the product I was selling. So if in the mid sixties you received one of these as a Christmas present, you no doubt will remember that it did indeed have the new wonder ingredient.

Another incident I recall was standing at Frodsham market, in Cheshire, this was situated in the High Street, Linda's brother, Terry, had come with me for the day. Terry would have been aged about twelve, I'd sneaked off somewhere, probably the pub, when I got back there had been a cloudburst, and half my stock was sailing down the High Street.

Working on the markets was a hard life, you would have to be onsite at the crack of dawn to stand any chance of a stall and even then you were governed by the weather. The market stalls were saturated with wallpaper, carpets and not with the weather with sellers. The Barrow in Furness and Ullswater markets involved stopovers, by the time you covered the accommodation, fuel and stall costs, I was out of pocket, so its goodbye to Cleveleys and back to good old Stoke on Trent, Bentilee actually.

Job 26 Bus Driver P.M.T. Clough Street Hanley

Before we go into the details of the job, this was the year 1968 that my only brother, Tommy, was killed in a road traffic accident, the date 10th, September. He was eighteen months younger than me, a tragic loss of life he was twenty-six, married, and father to an eighteen month old baby daughter, Michelle.

Back to the PMT, actually I went for a job at Bassett's as a coach driver and PMT as a service driver, both offered me a position, but the coach driving would have meant time away from home again. So I took the job with the PMT, and can honestly say that I never regretted it, the only drawback was, my temper.

I was often in trouble for fighting, but this was only when I got caught and reported. One of the more memorable occasions was on a late Saturday night turn, a stinker of a turn, main line, thirty minutes meal break taken at Longton Bus Station. I arrived at Longton more or less on time, as I drew in I could see that there was a Taxi parked on my stand, I gave him a blast on the horn which he ignored. I got out and remonstrated with him, he gave me an abusive reply, saying "Call yourself a driver…….." at that I jumped into the cab and put the bus on the stand, shunting his taxi onto the pavement, he came round to me and pulled my shirt, (which was a new one) and pulled a button off it, that was it, the red mist came down. The next thing I knew, was that I was been dragged off by fellow workmates, and his glasses was embedded in his nose.

I thought this is it, the sack, so why work on a Saturday night until midnight, however I was reassured that I wouldn't be reported, so I carried on. As soon as I got into the depot at the end of the shift, I was told that I had to report to Mr Crocker on

Monday morning, he was the gentleman based at Head Office and was in charge of all the drivers and a reputation as being strict but fair, so Monday morning came and there I was fearing the worst, I went in and gave him an honest account of what had happened. Mr Crocker confirmed that it was the taxi driver who had instigated the complaint and had made allegations of assault, however, and this was a surprise. Mr Crocker had told him if he was to make such an allegation, then the PMT would take action against him, for plying for hire on a bus stop, which could result in him loosing his hackney carriage driver's licence.

I was told in future to have more control on my temper, but to forget the incident, but he then said "Off the record and before you go, I would like to know, how you can push a car with a bus onto the pavement, without causing damage to either vehicle" I replied "Mr Crocker in the same vein and off the record, as a Blackpool bus driver you learn all the tricks".

Another time I had been reported for being off route, I had been spotted by the Chief Inspector, Charlie Cole; he had been returning from some late night function and had seen me in Burslem, sitting outside the Adulte ballroom. The bus had caught his attention, it was a relic from a takeover that was seldom used on anything other than Stone Local, and sure enough when he checked the work records it was allocated to Stone Local.

I was hauled before Mr Trivett, (Mr Crocker had retired), I explained (that's my excuse) that I was that ashamed of doing an eight hour shift and only bringing in the sum of six pound odd, that I had tried to get some additional revenue, He examined my waybill and commented that I had no entries for the last two or three trips, I said "Yes but I tried" and got away with it!

Congleton bus station was another memorable occasion, by this time I was a One Man Operator, (OMO for short). I had arrived at the bus station late as usual, booked the fares and attempted to pull away, the back nearside wheels caught the concrete bus shelter, demolishing it. I telephoned the garage, reporting I'd had an accident, they said "Have you knocked the shelter down", I said "no it fell down when I reversed out of it!" I was asked if the bus was serviceable, I confirmed it was, and was told to carry on, half way through the route, I rang them again, and said "I've changed my mind," explaining that as I'd gone round a bend, the rear nearside window complete with frame had fallen in, and two ladies were sitting there holding it!

Talking about OMO I had a brand new Daimler Roadliner centre door type, I was operating the Hanley-Barlaston service. As I approached Stoke, I braked and got into an uncontrollable wheel wobble, a collision was unavoidable. Luckily for me a young lady passenger, a resident of Barlaston volunteered herself as a witness, as she was stood at the front, as she had seen me struggling with the steering wheel.

Same service, different date, different bus, again a Roadliner but not the centre door type, it was winter and the bus had been broken down at Barlaston, the air tanks had frozen up. The mechanics had been out and sorted it out, and I was returning to Hanley via Blurton. As we came down the slight gradient, to what is now the A500 roundabout, on my nearside was a parked car, and on my right, two parked cars, as I proceeded through the gap, one of the cars on my right pulled out, causing me to brake. I skidded on the slush and ice, hit the car on my nearside and ended up in a wall, I had to leave the bus by the rear emergency exit, the driver of the car I'd collided with was in the dentists awaiting a tooth extraction, and was waiting for the injection to take effect. The Police arrived, who must have been having a bad day with the weather conditions as they were, the poor car driver who had done nothing wrong, was being questioned about the damage to his car. It was an Austin A40, as you can imagine a bus hitting it had caused considerable damage.

He told the Police Officer he thought it was a write off, at this the officer said, "Don't be silly, if your spark plugs want changing you don't throw the engine away!" I thought poor sod (the driver) we've got a right one here, anyway at this point a lady approached me and told me she had witnessed the accident and had got the registration number of the car that had caused it, fantastic.

Months later I was operating this run again, when I recognized the lady, and instead of taking her fare, thanked her, explained who I was and to sit down and have a free ride in appreciation. She was astounded that firstly, I remembered her and secondly that on that previous day she had a letter from the car drivers insurance, suggesting, that I was in fact the cause of the accident, apparently the registration number that she had supplied to the Police was a digit out, so no action could be taken by the insurance company against the third party.

They had tried to claim off the PMT as their client was blameless, the PMT agreed with them, but nevertheless their driver (me) had been proved to be not at fault, so the poor bloke lost all round, so the moral is always have full comprehensive insurance!

Again on this service we called at the Wedgwood factory, at Barlaston, on the return journey I had this obnoxious American lady complaining about the bus, again a Daimler Roadliner, back in the States she went on, their buses were this that and the other, I kindly informed the said lady, that Daimler was German, the engine was a Cummings, which was American, and the braking system was Westinghouse, which was American, however the seats may be British, she sat down and never spoke again, not even "Have a good Day".

At Clough Street it could only be described as a pleasure to go to work, quite a few of us socialized on our rest days, not just the drivers but their wives as well. In those days you had wives not partners, although one or two had girlfriends, some secret, some not!

We decided that we would form our own social club, which I think we called 'The Omnibus Club' but I'm not sure. I was the concert secretary and Vic Evans was the treasurer, it is very strange as I should get to this stage in the book, as today, 7th June 2012 I've attended Vic's funeral, he was seventy five, more about Vic later.

Every four weeks we used to have a social evening, always our shift, I would book a comedian and a group or a singer, and we had some fantastic nights, we would try and have different venues around the City, always using a working man's club. A couple of incidents come to mind, the first, I'd applied for a phone at home, as I'd left home, a telephone had been delivered complete with the disc in the middle stating our number Blythe Bridge **** I wrote it down, and off I went to work, that day I was on the Hanley – Buxton route, which took me out of the area for most of the day.

At Hanley Bus Station I'd bumped in to Vic, and gave him this number, I did explain that it was yet to be connected, but I don't think Vic heard me, anyway later that day Vic rang Linda. A female answered "Hello Blythe Bridge ****" to which Vic said "Hi Linda its Vic," the female said, "Linda? Sorry this is Mrs Knobbs"

Well Vic made numerous cracks about the name, before realising it was in fact not Linda, it was a firm of Plumbers in Forsbrook called Knobbs Plumbers, the number we had been given was in fact going to be, as was the norm in those days, a party line.

Another was a concert held at Smallthorne Victory Club, the comedian had failed to turn up, and the group had gone off for a break, so I fancied myself as a bit of a comedian, I thought there nothing to this, so I got up onto the stage, and started to tell a joke, now I knew I was dying on my feet, I put my hand onto what I believed to be a stool left behind by the musicians, but it was in fact a set of symbols. I fell into the drums causing great hilarity, there wasn't a dry eye in the house!

Staying with Vic, besides his job as a driver on the PMT, he decided to take over a pub, the Mostyn Arms, in Hanley. In those days under no circumstances were you allowed to enter licensed premises whilst working, so if we were on a late turn we used to meet up and go for a drink after we had finished our shifts. Pubs closed at ten thirty, however there was always the Potters Club in Hanley, which was the only place licensed to be open until two am, I'll tell you more about the Potters Club later.

On this particular occasion we had met up at the Mostyn Arms, as Vic was taking over the pub from his sister Gwen on this very day, and it was to be a farewell for Gwen and a welcoming party for Vic, anyway, it was turned midnight when we were raided by the Police for drinking after time. They started to take everyone's name, address, occupation etc. When they came to me, (remember this was before the breathalyser), they asked for my particulars, I was sitting there in my bus drivers uniform complete with two badges, red for driver, and green for Conductor, so I gave them my name and address, date of birth and then said "Guess" for occupation. The Police Officer said, "Well sir, you could be a driver or a conductor," I said "Wrong, Brain Surgeon," he just wrote it down and went to the next one.

Another driver had put his pint under the bench seat to hide it, the Police dog had found it and started to drink it, then the pubs phone rang, the Police Inspector answered it, the voice said, "Watch out you are going to be raided," the Police Officer said "How do you know?" the driver informed him that his girl friend had been involved in an accident and was at the Police station, and that he'd heard it over the Police radio. Remember in those day's we didn't have mobile phones, the Inspector politely informed him he was too late. I heard Vic say to the Police that it was a private party and nobody had paid for their drinks, at the same time as the guy, whose drink had been drunk by the Police dog, was complaining what the pint has cost him! Anyway, we didn't hear any more about the matter.

Another time, this was after I'd left the PMT, I was out driving one of my minibuses and I thought I'd pop in and see Vic, I pulled up outside the pub, and as I got out a young girl asked if I'd like a good time, I looked at her and thought, I've got a daughter your age, so I thought I'll play it along and said "Why, do you play dominoes?" The answer was unprintable, I told Vic, and he described her to a T, and now remember Vic's sense of humour was dry and he was quick witted, he said, "Ah yes he knew the girl but she was very shy!"

I laughed at this comment, saying something along the lines of I doubt it, no, he explained, when you asked about a game of dominoes, she couldn't count and probably thought I wanted a game of five's and three's.

As I've said work was a pleasure and we often played tricks on each other for instance, one day at Hanley Bus Station. I had had my meal and had gone to the toilet, I was sitting in the cubicle, minding my own business, when all of a sudden a lighted newspaper came over the top followed by water. I pulled my trousers up from around my ankles, and opened the door, just as Harry Walklet was running out laughing, I shouted "I'll get you!"

Months later we were at one of our social evenings, Harry was there with his wife, when I spied my chance, he had gone into the gents, so I followed him in, I stood next to him chatting. I then said "Harry can you remember that time in Hanley Bus Station," Yes" he laughingly replied, "Can you remember what I shouted after you?, I said I would get you, well whilst we've been standing at the trough, I've urinated over your shoes!" He came over to our table and showed Linda his soaking wet suede shoes.

Then we had Johnny Jackson, known to all as Bucket, one night I had arranged that we could gain free entrance to a night club, called the Penny Farthing, I knew the bouncer, and I'd told him that there would be about 10 of us. No problem except that we would not be allowed in wearing our uniform jackets, so we all made sure that we had suitable sweaters with us, but we didn't tell Johnny. He stood out like a sore thumb, if you were kind, you would say he was chubby; anyway, he looked decidedly out of place sporting his braces!

Another time after we had finished work and we all had been for a drink, one of our lot suggested going up to Keele Motorway Services, it would have been at least 1am. We all refused except Johnny and Derek Whitmore, well Derek was single, Johnny got home at about four in the morning, crept in and turned all the clocks back a couple of hours, as he got into bed, his wife was not at all impressed, went to his jacket, pulled out his pocket watch, yes, you've guessed it, the only one he hadn't altered, boy was he in trouble.

Let's talk now about the Potters Club, it was in fact a gambling club, I don't know if there was an entrance fee, but I knew the doorman, and he would let us in without charge. We would all meet up in the basement, when I say all of us, there would be about seven of us, the floors above were basically gambling rooms. Watching men on a Thursday or Friday night, still in their work clothes, throwing away their empty wage packets and then most probably going home to some poor wife and mother with no money to put food on the table, put me off gambling of any description for life.

The Potters Club also had another reputation, we were living with my Mother at the time, Mum asked Linda as to what time I finished, Linda said "About eleven pm", Mum said "Oh we might as well wait up for him," Linda replied "I think he's going for drink after work at some club in Hanley called the 'Potters' Club," Mum said "What! That's a knocking shop," (a place of ill repute) so as you can imagine I had one or two questions to answer when I got home. I denied that this was the case and to pacify Linda promised I would take her there the following week on my day off, which was a Wednesday. To be fair to me I had never been there on a Wednesday before, yes, you've guessed it, the place was full of ladies of the night. Another social club we had at Clough Street, was the Hen Pecked Husbands Club, yes Linda said I could join!

Back to the buses, they were now operating Double Deckers on pay as you enter, and they introduced a new system called Johnson Boxes. The idea was that passengers on boarding the bus would put their bus fare into this box. The box itself was glass sided, so that the driver could see the money, and then with a foot mounted switch he would drop the money into the cash vault. The system was meant to be correct fare only, no change to be given, and most importantly no tickets were issued, we always had a float, mainly copper. As far as the bus company was concerned it was a disaster, as far as drivers was concerned, it was a licence to print money, it got to the stage when if you had a turn on a run that operated Johnson Boxes, drivers would offer you cash to change duties.

Most passengers were completely flummoxed by the system, and nine times out of ten would offer the fare to the driver, who should tell them 'All fares in the box please' (note the word Should). There was a story going around about a woman boarding the bus in Bentilee, going to Longton, she got on the bus and said to the driver "Longton Please" the driver replied "in the box please," she looked at him, then on tip toe said into the box "Longton Please".

It was said that some drivers bought new cars even houses out of the proceeds, I even heard some unkind suggestion that I started my Taxi business from Johnson Boxes, I mean as if!

Forty years later in Glasgow I came across this system again, but on the fare being placed in the box, tickets were issued and it was correct fare only, my journey from the bus station was £1.35 but I only had a £10.00 note the driver said "Sorry no change" I explained I'd only got a £1.00 coin, which he accepted and watched me put it in the box, the ticket issued claimed I had in fact paid £1.35, he said "Don't worry other fares had tended too much".

Back to the PMT, they had a system of minimum fare on some of the routes that travelled through the city, it was to encourage people to use the other routes, as an example if you required to go to a point, say Burslem or Tunstall and say the fares to these destinations was five pence, the minimum fare was based on the fare of Kidsgrove, which was say ten pence, it was actually quite a good system because the services it was operating on were hourly and the others were every few minutes, anyway, what I'm coming to is, I was on the service Hanley – Congleton, minimum fare Kidsgrove.

When I got to Burslem a regular trouble maker attempted to board, I knew what was coming, because he wanted to travel a few miles only, as I said he had a reputation and an appearance to match, unshaven, roughly dressed, heavy drinker and about six foot two, as he got on he threw some coppers on to the cash tray, I tried to explain it was minimum fare only, at that he called me a Bastard, that was it, I jumped out of the cab, grabbed him, shoved the coppers in his mouth and threw him off. Much to my surprise, and others, he went off like a little church mouse, and never caused trouble again, he was nothing but a bully, who had been caught out.

Which brings me to another time when my temper got the better of me, and as I tell the story, it seems so childish, but here goes, at the time there was a practice called Wogging, which was basically following the bus in front and letting them do all the work, the main culprits were opposing garages, one of the prime areas was when the number three route, which operated between Meir and Talke Pitts, arrived in Tunstall and clashed with Route four ,Tunstall to Hanford, operated by Stoke garage. This route had the advantage as it started from Tower Square and could watch our arrival, then sit in behind us, the timetable from Tunstall was every four minutes, which meant a number three every eight minutes and the same with the number four.

On the day in question yours truly was on the number three, and low and behold the number four was waiting for us, now we were on time, so this meant that they were running late, and these were the days when the buses were well patronised, we were not only carrying our load but his, and boy was I getting worked up, every time I looked in the driving mirror I could see him, crawling along in the distance, sure enough when we arrived in Hanley, and by this time we were running late, because we were in effect carrying two loads, he attempted to pull round us, no chance, I jumped out, got hold of him, and he was a big bloke, and I thought to myself, don't hit him, because you'll get the sack so I dragged him out his cab and threw him down the bus, unfortunately for me by this action I'd trapped a woman behind the door, and she quite rightly complained, so I was immediately taken off service, and suspended, which resulted in appearing before Mr Trivett.

I was surprised to find that not only was I was appearing before Mr Trivett, but the other driver also. I was asked to explain my actions, which I attempted to, Mr Trivett exploded saying that I was dismissed, however I had the right to appeal within seven days, the following day we were scheduled to go on holiday for fourteen days in Tenby on a caravan holiday, so I merely said "That I couldn't" he exploded again saying "Yes it would be a waste of time, as he would not employ hooligans or thugs", so I thought I might as well thump this bloke now, after all I've got the sack!, but at that this driver asked for permission to speak, saying that everything I had said was true, and if it hadn't been for the fact of the woman being involved, the incident would have been forgotten, and that he was prepared to shake hands, so Mr Trivett changed my dismissal to a final warning.

I thought Stanton you have a wife and two children to support, at thirty two years of age to lose your job for fighting it's time you grew up, and surprisingly I did learn to control my temper, well most of the time.

One of the routes that I operated was Hanley to Lichfield, the following incidents are both related to this service, the first was on a Sunday morning. I had departed from Hanley late, due to a shortage of change, the bus was an AEC semi luxury, with a six speed gearbox, and they could fly. So there I was flying along the A34 towards Trentham, just before Trentham Gardens, on your left was the remainder of a bridge, it was just a wall, anyway as I drove past, lo and behold, a Radar Trap.

In those days, it was a box, positioned on the roadside with a Police Officer who radioed your speed through to another officer who was situated further up the road, the first thing I saw was the Police Officer with his hand up. I managed to stop, the officer said, "You know when I saw you coming I didn't think it was a PMT bus," (this was because it had a slightly different livery) so I came straight back, with the comment; "Why did you think it was BOAC" (the name of a defunct airline) his response was just as quick, "No Midland Red".

When I returned to the garage at the end of the shift, I reported this fact to the garage superintendent, Mr Steadman known to one and all, as Oker Steadman, (don't know why), he always had a fag in his mouth, I told him I'd been booked for speeding. He asked "What were you doing," when I told him sixty three he nearly swallowed his fag, saying "We haven't got a bus that goes that fast," my response was, "do me a favour then and ring up the police and tell them the radar was wrong!"

The other incident was of a far more serious nature, as I approached Rugeley, luckily driving at a moderate speed, a young man jumped in front of the bus, in an attempted suicide bid, I braked, at the same time throwing the bus towards the centre of the road, missing him by a fraction, I got out and proceeded in giving him a piece of my mind. I noticed that he was immaculately dressed, and that he was talking rubbish to me, something about Bananas. Rugeley Town Centre was only a couple of minutes away, so I called into the Police Station and reported the incident, the following day I was on the same turn, so I enquired at Rugeley Police Station about the previous night. The station officer explained that he was aware of the incident, and informed me that he had been taken into custody and admitted to St Georges Psychiatric Hospital, Stafford, for an overnight stay, and had since been released.

Bananas was central to the story, apparently, he was from a very well-to-do family; hence his dress sense, he was living on his own, and his gas cooker had developed a fault, he had gone into the gas showrooms, and they had told him, a repairman would attend in three days time, he would not accept this, telling them to take it out, which they did, hence the bananas, he had only eaten banana sandwiches for a week.

St George's got in touch with social services, who arranged for a electric cooker to be installed immediately, and he was back on track, the police officer commented on his actions saying, "It was probably only a half hearted attempt, a cry for help" but only I and a few passengers know the real story, he was lucky to be alive!

Linda and Tina rang me today, asking about directions to Market Drayton, this bought back memories to a couple of incidents when I was working as depot spare, essentially you were there to cover any missed turns (or if any driver failed to turn up for duty). There was four am spare, then five am, seven am & one pm, potentially there could've been four drivers sitting there waiting for something to do, it never happened though! If you were lucky and all the drivers turned in, you sat around for seven hours; otherwise you had to cover whatever turn that came up.

While we are on the subject of spare drivers, I can recall an incident involving the permanent 4am spare driver, his duty was to turn up at 4am Monday-Friday to cover any missing turn at Hanley garage. The day previous he must have been approaching his 60th birthday, as was the law to renew his PSV licence he had to have a medical to declare him fit to drive, he passed the medical and turned up for work the following morning as per norm. He again, as the norm made himself comfortable & had a sleep whilst awaiting a missed turn. Sure enough a missed turn happened, when he was approached it was found to everyone's horror that he was in fact dead.

Going back to spare drivers the first incident I want to talk about was when I was the one pm spare, it was a private hire, Mucklestone Races, now I am not, and never have been interested in horse racing, plus I'd never heard of Mucklestone Races, no problem Bill, it's only point to point and it's near to Loggerheads, so off I went following the directions as per the detailed itinerary. All went well until I arrived at Mucklestone. I followed the signs at Mucklestone Church, right to the race meeting, I drove up this lane which was getting narrower by the yard, it was that narrow I had to pull the driving mirror in, but I had no choice but to keep on going. The passengers reassured me I was on the right road, anyway, eventually I came to the entrance, which was a gate entrance to a field, and there was this bloke demanding a five pound car parking fee, I laughed at him, telling him, I hadn't got that kind of money. I couldn't go back as the lane was full of traffic, plus another PMT bus had followed me, so he had no choice but to let me in for free, apparently it was a free course for spectators, but parking was payable.

Eventually the other PMT driver came to me, he had paid the parking fee, I know you will be thinking five pound is nothing, but this was about 1972 and my wages were less than eighteen pounds per week, anyway, I had a chat with the other driver, who was worried about claiming his parking ticket, when I hadn't paid. This matter was solved by me having a walk round the car park, and removing (sounds better than pinching) a car park ticket from the windscreen of a sports car, we split the money between us, in fact we did bump into another PMT driver at the races, who informed us that buses parked up at the church, well no one had told us.

The other incident was in same area, only on this day I fell for a Newcastle depot turn, Market Drayton local, operated on Wednesdays only, I told them I hadn't a clue on the area, no problem was the answer: a) you have a detailed running board and b) the passengers will direct you, so Market Drayton to Newport, the running board instructions were to terminate at some farm on the outskirts of Newport, this was alright until I ran out of passengers, no one on the bus and still about fifteen minutes running time left, I never did find the terminus, or the correct way back.

On my return to Market Drayton it was time for my meal break, I had asked the previous passengers on the availability of food, and was recommended to try the Market Hall. So I parked the bus up, and made my way to what I thought was the Market Hall. I walked round the building trying to find the entrance, when I was approached by a uniformed guard, asking if he could help me, I explained to him I was trying to find the entrance as I was hungry and was trying to buy something to eat, he laughed informing me I was trying to get into, wait for it!!! A CORSET factory! However, he did give directions to the Market Hall.

Another amusing incident, the PMT used to run a service to Blackpool on holiday periods, and on this occasion myself and a friend Johnny Mountford, were on the Blackpool Expresses, neither of us had any passengers for the return journey, so we went to my former home in Cleveleys, as I'd left a garden shed there. It was already dismantled ready for the journey back to Stoke, well, we tried all ways to get this shed into our two buses, if we got the roof in, the side wouldn't go in, and if we got the back in the front wouldn't go in, we tried all angles without success, but the neighbours had a good laugh!

Again on holiday periods only, the PMT had several holiday destination routes, I seemed to drop for the Scarborough one. The first time I did it, the route took you over a Toll Bridge at Selby, I was terrified, the bridge seemed to be moving as you drove across it. When I got to the other side, there was this bloke asking me for ten bob (fifty pence), I told him to get lost; I wanted paying to drive over it!

On my arrival in Scarborough, I had to have eight hours off, before returning empty. I rang the Tours Department at Stoke, and asked if I had to return the same route, "Yes", was the reply, I told them "if that's the case they had to send another driver up, I'm coming back on the train!", they relented and said, "If I knew another route it would be o.k." and from then on Selby was by-passed. (The bridge was over the River Ouse, and I know now that the feeling of the bridge moving was caused by the bridge being a swing bridge, that swung out from the centre, and instead of opening up, it in fact swung out sideways!).

Today Thursday 24th January 2013, we have just had six days of snow, and the promise of more to come, anyway this jogged my memory back to the days of real snow and one day in particular. I was driving on the Hanley–Buxton route, one man operated, the shift involved two trips to Buxton, on the first trip into Buxton, I had an AEC semi-luxury bus. As I approached Flash, I encountered very strong winds, the bus had on the lower half of the body, both sides, hinged access panels, this was the access to the engine, but the wind was that strong, the panels would not stay down, I appeared to have wings. Obviously I could not carry on as the bus was taking up most of the road, I had to have a Police escort into Buxton Bus Station, I then made my way to the North Western Bus Depot, and they loaned me one of theirs, (same firm different name).

On my second trip I left Hanley and as I approached Cobridge traffic lights, I was in the faster moving outside lane, when without warning a car pulled out straight in front of me, I stood on the brakes and managed to avoid a collision, the car driver apologised. I noted his registration number and enquired with the passengers for any injuries, the only comments were from frustrated passengers collecting goods from their shopping bags, they all agreed that I was not at fault. On arrival at Buxton, as previously arranged I changed buses, they had temporally welded the side panels down, and I then returned to Hanley using my original bus.

It must have about four months later when I had a phone call relating to this incident from the PMT's insurance officer, who asked me if I could recall the incident, I told them what I could remember, they then said "I don't suppose you have the car registration number" to their amazement I had it to hand, but as I explained to them it was luck, as I'd written down the number on my Bus Fare Table, and bus fares were due to go up in another two weeks time, had they left it till then I would have disposed of the old fare book.

He went on to explain that a female passenger was claiming for a dislocated shoulder, she had stated the facts that I was not at fault, as the car driver had caused the incident, the confusion was caused by the fact that I was driving a North Western bus, and this service, Hanley Buxton, was in fact a joint service with North Western. Just to finish the tale off relating to this service, I've seen the time in winter when on the return journey from Buxton the snow was so bad that to allow passengers to alight, I've slowed down, to as slow as I dared without actually stopping, and they have had to jump from the moving bus, but I can never recall collecting passengers in these conditions!

I was asked to do a seven day camping holiday with the boy scout's, to Brixham, the only downside to it, instead of the usual two hundred mile allowance for trips out, this tour was only allowed one hundred once you were there for sightseeing trips. On arrival at the camp site, and after a struggle I managed to get the coach into the camp, the next morning the campsite manager made himself known to us, and asked if I was the driver, thinking I had perhaps parked in the wrong position. I enquired what was wrong, he replied "Nothing, it's just that you're the first driver to get a coach in!" no wonder I'd struggled to get it in, and I've got the same manoeuvres to get out.

Anyway we were there for the week, and I've only got one hundred miles to play with, so on one day I drove into Torquay to refuel, which was a half day out for them, no mileage claim, and another half day taking the bus to be washed. For the full day out they wanted to go to Plymouth. I could not do it there and back in the allocated miles, but studying the map, I thought if I went over Dartmoor, then return via the main roads, I'd just about do it, so off we set, my map didn't say anything about narrow roads.

I saw the sign that stated 'No left turns for Lorry's,' but it didn't say anything about buses, so I turned, eventually, I came to a bridge. I thought I won't get through, but I did, feeling confident I carried on, till I came to another narrow bridge, same thoughts, but this time I was correct. I couldn't get through, well not without damaging the coach.

When you are proceeding through a gap and both sides of your vehicle are catching, you know its tight, there was even spectators standing on the bridge walls, filming it, and when I finally got through, I had a round of applause, all very embarrassing.

On arrival in Plymouth you are constantly harassed to take your passengers down to the dockyard, and onto a boat trip. I played the touts against each other for the best rate, ending up with a £1.00 per head, thirty six children and about five adults, only the question about how many children I had on board wasn't asked, only how many passengers. So when they got onto the boat, it was five at £2.00 and thirty six at £1.50, nice earner for Bill. I of course couldn't be found till later.

I was in fact embroiled in an argument in the local Royal Blues Bus Company canteen, with the local drivers and telling them about the trouble encountered over the bridge, they smiled and said, "We know how you feel we have to come over that bridge on a regular bus route" I fell for it, saying it was impossible without damaging the bus, after much huffing and puffing, they let me into the secret, the buses they used were seven foot six wide against mine at eight foot two.

But, my troubles weren't over, on the final night, a storm like no other blew up, the tents were blown away, and at three o'clock in the morning I attempted to open the boot of the coach, this was to try and keep the food dry, which was open to the elements. As I opened the boot lid, the wind tore it off its hinges. Everybody's belongings were scattered far and wide, I found my suitcase in another field, there was also a disused tractor that had been blown on to its side. The Scout leaders placed the gas cookers inside the coach in an attempt to dry some personal clothes.

I had arranged for Linda to collect me from the PMT garage at Stoke on my return, as I drew up the smile on her face, said, look at him showing off his tan, I was driving wearing short's and a jumper, they were the only dry clothes I had! All the way back we were listening to the radio news, about a missing boat from the Royal Naval College, Dartmouth that had been caught in the same storm, I think they claimed it was a force ten, thankfully they were all safe.

The PMT were not impressed on the state of their coach, the boot tied up with string and both side panels damaged! Linda and I were later both invited to the scout meeting and the video of the coach going over the bridge was well received.

It was with memories of this trip that this next tale centres on, at the time I was off work with a back problem. I received a telephone call asking if I would be interested in a forthcoming week's tour for some boy scouts, I said "Sorry, but I am at present not at work due to illness," they said "well we have spoken to your employer, who stressed that you have experience in this type of work, and that you would be prepared to sleep under canvas, and in fact that sleeping on a hard surface could actually help my back, would I please consider it?" "Yes" I said "I'll think it over and give you a ring back"

What I hadn't realised was that it was a wind up, that my mates had conjured up, we all had a good laugh especially as I'd fallen for it. So I thought to myself its pay back time. The main culprit was Ron, aided and abetted by Arthur, I purchased the magazine Exchange & Mart, and filled in and sent off every coupon I could find, before long they were inundated with catalogues, application forms to join the Army, Navy, RAF, Prison service, remedies for flat feet, keep fit exercises, gym equipment, foreign language courses, book clubs even the Encyclopaedia Britannia. I can remember Ron saying the Postman was laughing even before he rang the doorbell.

One day I got my Mother in on the act, we telephoned him claiming to be a transport company with a load of tiles, when would it be suitable for delivery? Ron said, "I'm glad you rang could you please redirect them, giving my address," I was listening in on the extension, and started laughing.

In the late sixty's early seventy's, Sunday evening tours were very popular, you would depart from say Hanley, at about six pm, take a very leisurely drive around the countryside and stop at a little country pub, or a rural town, like Newport. The one I can recall doing was advertised as the Goyt valley, out via Congleton and Macclesfield, we had a detailed itinerary, which was alright until we reached the outskirts of Macclesfield. My itinerary read: 'After leaving Macclesfield take the A537 then after two point seven miles turn left for the Goyt Valley', the problem was, the speedometer on my bus didn't work, so I took the A523 and took them to Rudyard Lake, well they enjoyed it and I don't think they knew any different.

Job 27 Driving Instructor.

As much as I enjoyed working at the PMT, it was not a well paid job, and I had a wife and two small children who needed feeding and clothing etc. so to supplement my income I put an advert in the local evening paper, offering to give driving lessons to learner drivers in their own cars. My first success was a close neighbour; she had previously failed her test four times, but got through after having tuition from me.

Then there was a lady from Trentham, her car was an Austin A35, I arrived one day as arranged, no car in the drive, I thought strange, I knocked on the door, at that she came out looking very flustered, apparently she had tried to turn the car round on the back lawn, and had failed. It was stuck in the rose bushes!, she said "Would you push whilst I tried to steer it out," I said, "No you push, I'll get it out," and out it came.

Horace, was a fellow worker on the PMT, a conductor, he hadn't got a car, so I gave him lessons in mine, I should add that mine, was a Van, a Vauxhall Viva. Horace really struggled with clutch control, however overnight, he mastered it, I congratulated him, his reply amused me, he had realised that the pedals were similar to a piano, and he had practised on his piano, at home, well it worked for him. Horace and I were out one day practising reversing, we shot back through someone's privet hedge, well through, is an exaggeration, more like into.

It was about this time that the government started to make noises about Driving Instructors having to become registered, so I gave it up, you can tell how good I was I took Linda (the wife) out on a driving lesson on a Sunday and we never spoke again until Tuesday!

Job 28 Labouring at Blythe Colours & Mister Kipling.

Money was still in short supply so during the winter months when work was quiet, I did work for an Agency, this was on my rest days. There were two jobs that I can recall; one was at a bakery at Trent Vale, and the other Blythe Colours at Cresswell.

At that time the Bakery was called Champion Bread, now of course it's Mister Kipling. The work was nights, cleaning the ovens, it was the most boring job I have ever done, in fact one night I fell asleep on a ladder. The only good thing was I could purchase cakes at greatly reduced prices and the money was good. The other job was at Blythe Colours, Cresswell, this was shovelling clay into large wheelbarrows, not a nice job, but hey ho I got paid for it.

Job 29 Petrol Attendant.

What can I tell you about this job, in short not a lot, these were the days before self service, customers would pull up, and tell you to either fill it up, or say a gallon or perhaps a £1.00's worth, you would serve them and ask if they wanted the windscreen cleaning or did they want the car's engine oil checking. I was actually still employed at the PMT bus but was off work, sick, and this job was casual, cash in hand, the job was short lived but the cash was welcome.

As you can imagine I was always looking for ways to earn extra cash, as we simply couldn't exist on my wages, so I started doing a bit of taxi work, strictly pirating at first, but it gradually built up so that I could make a reasonable amount of extra money.

Job 30 & 31 Taxi Driver/Coach Operator

B.Cabs Taxi Services then I changed its name to: B.C. Travel. Well where do I start, it was 1972; I lived in Blythe Bridge which was a semi rural area, and it had no taxi service, so I spotted an opportunity. I had built it up whilst still working on the PMT, which could be tiring especially on this particular night. It started snowing about eight pm, and soon became a blizzard. I had gone to bed about nine 'o clock because nothing was moving, when we had a phone call from this guy, who apparently was a ships radio operator, he had gone to the Railway Station, but all trains had been cancelled, and it was essential that he got back to his ship at Hull. I agreed to attempt the journey and pleased to say, succeeded but what a journey, not only diversions but all the road signs were covered with snow, no sat navs, just instinct and a map, I got back at six am, just in time for a wash in cold water and then start my early shift bus driving. If I'd taken the day off it would have meant I'd worked all night for nothing.

I approached a friend, Bill Bloor, a fellow bus driver giving him the opportunity to come in with me, he declined but loaned me three hundred pounds to purchase a second car, Bill often says that I paid him back twice, and regretted not taking up the offer.

I approached a women's prison, Moor Court Prison at Oakamoor, and was offered the chance to tender for their work, which I was successful in, so it was time to part company with the PMT. I gained contracts with Staffordshire County Council transporting children with special needs, and was recommended for the Prison work at Werrington Detention Centre, which again was gained on Tender, so in a very short time I was operating a fleet of six Ford Granada's, all painted White, they did Prison work Monday – Friday, and on Saturdays, they did Weddings.

We were one of the first to operate White Wedding cars in the Stoke on Trent area, Linda passed her driving test in the morning and I had her doing a taxi job that day, the fare was only fifty pence but he gave her a pound telling her to keep the change, and then the cheeky so & so, rang me up and asked if it was my daughter!

My first employee was an ex-workmate from PMT days, Arthur. He had left the PMT because of health problems, this enabled Linda and I to have our first foreign holiday, a week in Majorca with Stoke on Trent Licensed Taxi Proprietors Association, this was taken every January to recuperate after the Christmas and New Year period. Leaving Arthur in charge, on our return, Arthur said, "Bill I don't know how you do it, any longer it would have killed me!" Sadly within the week he suffered an angina attack and died at the age of thirty two, leaving a wife and two young daughters.

I had made enquires as to the possibility of obtaining Hackney carriage licences, and was told that the only way, was to purchase existing licences from an operator wishing to sell, at I may add, an inflated price. However after making representations to Stoke on Trent City Council I was awarded two licences along with two new ranks, one at Blurton and the other Meir. Neither rank's did anything, however it gave us the opportunity to ply for hire in the city. To say the ranks didn't do anything wouldn't be strictly true, we were approached only once, it was midday on the Meir taxi rank, and the fare wanted to go to Perth in Scotland, but we couldn't do it as we had schools to cover.

I bought two Ford Cortina's for the taxi work, I also bought my first brand new car, it was a Peugeot 504 saloon car. I collected it from Hartshill Autos in Fenton, and on the way home from the dealers it broke down in Blythe Bridge, I couldn't believe it, I spent a couple of minutes just walking around it, it was brand new after all!

The next acquisitions were two LWB Humber Pullman Imperial limousines to use as Wedding Cars, well I actually bought them with bookings from Clarke's Taxis in Stoke, and it wasn't until I sold them that I found out that one of them was Diana Dors (a film star in the fifties and sixties) personal car, in the log book it just said Rank films, however I did see the car in a film, but can't remember which film it was.

Whilst we are on the subject of wedding's, let me tell you about a couple that we did, the first was taking the bride to the wrong church, (apparently there are two church's in the Meir), another one, I was still at Leek on a Wedding, when I should have been in Barlaston picking up the bride on another wedding. Fortunately the Driver on the Barlaston wedding, who was scheduled just to take the bridesmaids, realised that I was missing doubled back and did both runs, (what a blessing mobile phones would have been then).

Another occasion I took two weddings on, half an hour apart, they were both in the Meir, this was the one where I took the bride to the wrong church, they had told me it was the Church with steps in front, unfortunately both churches had steps, but as I said to the bride "Take your pick, which groom do you want" I should add that the error was realised before the bride got out of the car.

Then there was the time I had picked the bride and father up from an address in Trentham, as I drove past the Hem Heath pit (where the Hem Heath Hungry Horse pub is now at Trentham), I dropped behind an Army Truck towing a gun. I passed a comment about I'd better get past this vehicle as people may think it's a shot gun wedding, one look in the interior mirror, told me I'd hit a raw spot! Oops, Linda hated me taking Wedding Bookings, I can't think why!

It was about this point that we started experiencing problems with the telephone system, I was having men sitting around at night with no fresh calls coming in. I asked British Telecom or as it was known as BT to check to see if there was a fault, customers were telling me that we were constantly engaged, BT reported back that there was no problem, so I wrote to the Evening Sentinel, who sent a reporter to interview me. I explained the problem, and was asked, did I think it could be rivals, ringing in then leaving the phone off the hook, I replied

"No, not really, but I suppose it could be a possibility," the following night the Headlines read "Local taxi Proprietor accuses rivals of Sabotage"

I had only just joined the Stoke on Trent Taxi Drivers Association, and was joining them on a holiday to Spain, so I had a lot of explaining to do, luckily they believed me, but due to the publicity the Sentinel story generated, BT found out that there was a fault after all, it was in the Blythe Bridge telephone exchange, if two calls came in quick succession then it tripped out.

The holiday was a great success, and we had many more, and made many friends who we still meet from time to time, even now over forty years ago!

Moor Court Prison: I received a call on one occasion requesting that due to the nature of the escort, (a prisoners father had been a Professor of Oriental Studies at Cambridge University and it was his funeral) could we please supply the Blue Cortina, as it would be less conspicuous in the funeral procession. I refused explaining that the Cortina's were purchased for local Taxi Rank work, but promised to try and blend in. On arrival at Cambridge we were surprised to see that the funeral cars were in fact white. Our white Granada was the perfect match; apparently white is the colour of mourning in Asia.

I must admit that I was one of those who has often said that prisoners had it soft, like three meals a day, television etc, but at least on two occasions it was bought home to me that the one thing they didn't have, was their freedom. On both occasions they were emergency callouts, the first involved a prisoners daughter who was in a mental institution, aged unknown, but had a terminal illness, the mother was told that next time she saw her child it would be for the funeral, I can't really remember the location of the hospital, but I can remember that on the return journey the prisoner never spoke a word. The other time was a house fire in the Birmingham area, two of the prisoner's close relatives had died. On this occasion, I do believe that she was granted compassion leave.

What surprised me about this job was that the fire happened late at night, at about 1 am, the Police came to my house and knocked me up, they had been asked by the prison to notify me. Now out of hours, I had an ex-directory telephone number however the prison couldn't find it, they had rang BT explaining who they were and the circumstances but BT refused to divulge the number.

I saw some really sad cases like the University graduate who was in her early twenty's that I had to take to Holloway to die; this was due to drug misuse. I remember thinking what a pretty girl she had been, even though her complexion was yellow.

We had laughs as well, like the young woman who was coming up for release, I passed some comment to her about her future love life, and she replied "Bill I'd rather do press-ups on a cucumber patch".

There was another prisoner who was absolutely beautiful not only a pretty face, but she had the body to drool over. Obviously we got to know them as we had to take them on the routine appointments like opticians, dentists, doctors, etc. I should add that they were always with a Prison Officer, anyway she was also coming up for release, the big day came, I picked her up, no escort was on release. I joked with her that the wife had stopped my pocket money, she replied, "Bill I only go with men for money, for real love I prefer women!" I thought what a waste; by now you will have worked out she was a prostitute.

It was often claimed that Christine Keeler was in Moor Court, but I doubt it, however, I did convey Mary Bell back to the prison, the Child murderer from Derby Police station, after she had absconded from Moor Court. I remember the Governor being more concerned about what the public would do to her, as she was considered harmless by the powers that be.

My first escort to Holloway Prison was to take a violent female, who for the journey had been heavily sedated, the car stank of Largactil, she was sandwiched in the rear with a Prison Officer at one side of her, whilst on the other side were the prison's nurse, and another officer in the front.

As I arrived in London, remember no satellite navigation devices in those days, I thought I'd better ask for directions, I came to a Police Officer on point duty, pulled up, and feeling important shouted "Prison Escort, can you give me directions to Holloway Prison" my first surprise was that he was broad Scottish, the second of his directions, turn left, and ask again. Turn left wasn't really an option, as I was in the outside lane of four or five lanes of traffic, if I remember correctly we drove past Swiss Cottage four times.

I was asked one day by a female officer if I knew what the HMP on their uniforms stood for? Surprisingly my version of Hot Meat Pie's was not accepted, but then again I did not accept her version, which was, Honesty, Modesty, and Purity. Before we leave Moor Court let me tell you about a woman driver I employed, Joyce, who for some reason always wore a wig. On this particular day she had been on an escort to Holloway, on the return journey travelling on the M1 the Prison Officer's became concerned about a noise coming from the car, it was in fact the cars inner sill (Hillman Minx, rot boxes) that had come adrift and was dragging on the road.

Joyce was ignoring the noise but at the officers concerns, pulled on to the hard shoulder, to investigate, as she got out of the car, a lorry came past and her wig got caught up in it's slip stream, and much to the officer's amusement Joyce had to chase along the hard shoulder to retrieve her lost hair piece.

Werrington Detention Centre: It had mainly a catchment area of North Wales to Liverpool and all points in between. In the main we took prisoners for further court appearances. Once we had deposited the officers and the prisoner at the court, the day was ours, however, you couldn't go far as you never knew when your case would come up, so you tended to hang around the court. If we were still there at the lunch recession the officers and I would make our way to a café, I would always try and stand or sit between the two officers, as the café assistants would usually feel sorry for me, and which usually resulted in more on my plate than theirs.

On one occasion I went to the toilets and some bloke slipped me a packet of cigarettes, I have never smoked so the officers enjoyed them. Occasionally we had to do collections/transfers to the Risley Remand Centre, now that was a grim foreboding place. Even Linda was no stranger to Strangeways or Walton Gaol, on one of her visit's the accompanying officer whilst having lunch in the canteen advised her to check her salad for caterpillars or for glass, as this was a common addition.

The only time I can remember that we had to collect a prisoner direct from the courts, was a young lad, from Kidsgrove magistrate's court. As he sat in the back with an officer each side of him, one of the officer's asked him "What are you in for" this question surprised me as they are briefed before hand, the lad said "Stealing a Car" the officer bellowed at him, "You call me Sir, do you understand" "Yes Sir" the poor lad answered. The officer then went into great detail about how much the lad would enjoy his stay, and that he himself would make sure that he would enjoy it, because lad he thundered "that car you stole was my brothers" I should hasten to comment this was an exception to the rule.

Another regular run we did from there was taking the young lads to the VD (sexual health) clinic in Shelton, I had to park up in a side street opposite the clinic so that I could observe when my party was ready, but of course I could also see who was coming and going, and yes, I had one or two surprise recognitions.

The Medical Officer (MO) was at times, or it appeared to me, to be rather hard at times on the lad's, as an example we had an attempted suicide, which was more like a cry for help. The lad had cut his wrist, which had to be stitched, he was then transferred to another unit, the MO put the handcuffs over the stitches, complaining about this interfering with his leisure time.

I had been on an escort to somewhere in Mid Wales, on this occasion it was an appeal, which the inmate won. This meant an immediate discharge, as we were travelling back, one of the two Prison Officer's discovered that he had still got the cell key, how on earth he was not aware of the key in his jacket, was a mystery. It must have been at least nine inches of solid steel, so it was a turn around and back to the medieval police cells.

Again on an escort job, can't remember where, but I can remember that it was the Grand National Race day, and the two officer's asked me to place a bet on for them, you can't tell them that you don't know how to, do you? So I went wandering off, to find a betting shop, which of course I duly did.

I went into this rather crowded shop, and wandered around peeping at other punters betting slips, I soon got the gist of it, and placed the bets. Why am I telling you this I hear you ask, well, the comical part was I had been trying to look inconspicuous, that I hadn't looked where the exit was, there's me, Mr Cool having to ask "How do I get out?"

Another regular run we operated was once a week, we had to take their wage clerk to the bank, on this occasion, our car had broken down in the Detention Centre yard, so I sent another car out to do the job, whilst I organised recovery. At the time I was using a Blythe Bridge based mobile mechanic, Derek Dawson (more on him later), Derek picked me up and off we set, he had a Austin J2 pick up truck, and he drove like a man possessed, but it was his truck, what can I say, or do, besides hang on for grim death.

All of a sudden we are off the road, bouncing up the embankment, and him laughing hysterically, my seat was on fire! There were flames leaping around my backside, what had happened was that the passenger seat was hinged, I had got in and put the seat back into the upright position, the seat back upholstery was torn, and the seat metal backing had slid down and made contact with the battery. He soon extinguished the fire, and it didn't slow him down any.

The detention centres regime reminded me of army life, running up and down and standing to attention, in other words, discipline. Hot weather and Bank Holidays was a sure sign of trouble, either at Moor Court or Werrington, but thankfully never both at the same time.

Stafford Prison: I also had the coach contract at Stafford Prison, this consisted in the main of transporting prisoners from Stafford to the area workshops at Cold Meece, and two coaches were required, five days a week. On one occasion one of the coaches was involved in a collision with a car, in next to no time we had a very generous Police attendance, my driver was not at fault. However the police commented on the fact that every prisoner had volunteered themselves as witnesses, which was explained as being a day out for them.

The strange thing about this accident was that the previous Sunday morning, I had been taking the Prisoners from Moor Court Prison to Church in Cheadle, and had been involved in a collision with a car, two accidents in a few days, and both carrying Prisoners was uncanny. I decided to buy a twelve seater minibus, but it never moved a wheel for about ten months, so I decided to sell it, as the only use it had had was when we went on a camping holiday in it. Suddenly though it took off, in a very short space of time it was taking a group of ladies to and from the Staffordshire Potteries factory, not a great distance but it least it was a start, and then it was hired on a contract with Blythe Colours at Cresswell, to convey the evening shift of cleaners, again to and from the factory, only a small job, but it meant that the vehicle was getting noticed. There used to be a night club in Hanley called Top Rank, it was for the younger generation. I think it closed at midnight, anyway, at weekends I would put the minibus on at the end, charging fifty pence per person regardless of where they were travelling to in the direction of Cheadle. It soon got very popular, I've seen the occasion when it's pulled away with thirty-odd bodies on, the Police would watch us load up, but we were taking trouble off the streets, so they didn't bother us.

How the system worked was, that they had to pay as they left the bus, one clever dick shouted up the bus "Bill what are you going to do now, I'm getting out of the back doors, at my stop" I shouted back "Give you a medal, I've taken the handle off" all strictly illegal, but they weren't bothered it was a cheap way of getting home, and profitable for me, so, winners all round. The minibus was on a job at Leeds at the Headingly Stadium, it was an International Cricket game. When the party were ready to depart, the driver, found that he had a front wheel puncture, he tried but he couldn't get the wheel off, neither could the AA. We had to take the wheel off another Transit, complete with the Hub, travel to Leeds and change the complete assembly, as you can imagine it was the early hours in the morning when he got back. That very same morning I had a visit from the Police, about this Minibus, the previous night my Minibus had been seen acting suspiciously in the Leeds area, I explained about the breakdown, and they went away satisfied. The cricket pitch apparently had been vandalised, 'free George Davis' was the cause, and it was in 1975, I know because Google tells me!

We even picked up Brian Clough, the manager of Nottingham Forest Football Club, he was dubbed 'The Greatest Football Manager that England never had,' his car had broken down in Blythe Bridge and his team was playing at Port Vale. I also collected Norman Hartnell (the Queens Dressmaker) from Stoke Railway Station and delivered him to Lewis's Hanley, I asked him for his autograph he jokingly replied "Certainly, I charge a hundred pound," I replied, in the same vein, "That's no problem, it'll be charged to Lewis's!"

Can you remember Jollees Nightclub in Longton? The compere, Mel Scholes, shared a house with the singer Wendy Riley, and they had an account with us. Wendy was a lovely friendly lady, but Mel was totally opposite to his stage persona, it wasn't that he was unfriendly it was just that by nature he was the complete opposite to his stage presence.

Talking about Jollees, we had a certain customer, Joe he was a publican who when sober, was a gentle giant, but in drink he was the most awkward and unreasonable person you could have the misfortune to meet. He also had an account with us, as we also took his staff home after work, but this night I took him to Jollees, after the pub had closed. Some big star was topping the bill, I think it was Frankie Vaughan, I told him that it was admittance by ticket only, as it was a sell out, he said, "I'll bet you that I'll get in," I replied saying, "Ten pound says you don't," so we shook on it, as soon as I pulled up outside Jollees I said to the doorman (a mate) "Five pound for you if you don't let him in," so he didn't get in, and myself and the doorman had five pounds each.

As I said, this particular publican could be so irate in drink, one night he was driving home, drunk, and ran into the back of a lorry, the driver got out and recognized him, and said, "Joe, you're drunk, bugger off before the Police get here," Joe replied saying, "I'm not drunk, I'm going nowhere," result, a driving ban and a hefty fine! Then there was Fred, the licensee of the Duke of Wellington, now he was a real character, I have never seen anybody drink like Fred, on a rare night out, Linda and I were at Jollees (we must have had some free tickets) we bumped into Fred, so we sat and had a couple of drinks with him, when the waitress, who must have been known to me, approached me asking "If I had any part time driving vacancies", I said, "No sorry, but my friend here is a publican, "Fred have you any part time jobs?" she asked. He looked the girl straight in the eye, and said, "No because if you do a turn Dorothy (Wife) will sack you, and if you don't I'll sack you!"

I had instructions to pick Fred up from home, the Duke of Wellington, and take him to Stoke Station, I should add that Fred was an ex-Navy man and was terrified of flying, which explained why he was a cruise fanatic, as he got in the taxi, Dorothy said, "Fred have a nice holiday, have you got your money, got your travellers cheques?" "Yes" was the reply, as I drove away I enquired "What time is your train Fred?" "Train" he laughed, "Take me to the Grand Hotel Hanley." I laughed and mimicked Dorothy "Travellers Cheques?" the reply from Fred was, "Prostitutes accept them!"

Another time Fred and another local character Johnny Rice, went on a cruise together, on their return, I asked Johnny if had enjoyed the holiday? He said "Never again," they had called at Russia and the only thing he could remember about the place was that the streets were narrow, because he was bouncing off the sides of the walls. He told me about Fred's drinking, saying that "Fred would be drinking all day, carried to bed at about 3 am, and at 5 am, he was cleaning his teeth and whistling ready to start again."

Whenever you bought Fred home he was drunk, this night he had been to Jollees, I got him out of the car, which believe me was no small feat, I took him to the door, and placed him inside, and turned away. As I did, the door swung back hitting Fred and knocked him back outside, the problem was, BT had dug the pavement up, well laugh, Fred's in the hole and Dorothy was hanging out of the upstairs window shouting, "Leave him there," all this going on at about 2 am in the morning.

I also had the contract at the Apollo nightclub in Longton, this was 1974, previously in 1960 it was called the Cameo, and Linda and I had met there, the contract was to take the staff home in the early hours at a preferential rate, in return I was the sole provider of taxis to the customers, it was a system that worked quite well, and was beneficial to both of us.

I wonder if my son can remember this, one day they were low on beer, so I was used to fetch fresh stock for the bar, it would have been a Saturday morning, Keith was with me, he would have been aged about eight, and had wandered off into the toilets and came back asking for some coins so that he could play on the machines, it transpired he was on about the Condom machines!

I knew the manager, Fred Hampton, in fact his brother Eric had worked for me at one time, well until I sacked him, anyway, this particular night the artiste was a stripper performing with a snake, her act involved placing the snake in her private parts, and then putting the snake into the audiences faces, Fred and I were at the back watching. Well, Fred was watching, I was waiting for fares, that's my excuse and I'm sticking to it, she made as if she was going to approach us, Fred and I fell over each other trying to get out!

Thursday night at the Apollo was to coin a phrase, 'Queers Night', to me they were pound notes, and while it lasted I made a lot of money out of them. I got on great with them; after all they are some mother's sons! They had names for each other, there was Mother because he was the oldest, Daisy he lived on a farm, Michelle was Michael, Paul was Pauline and Philip was Phyllis. I've left Phyllis to the last to explain, Linda and I went shopping for a new three piece suite, at the Co-op in Cheadle, and lo and behold there's Phyllis, I said "Ay up Phyllis," no answer, on the Thursday night as soon as he saw me, he said "Oh Bill I could have died, at work I'm Philip," I replied, "If you're Phyllis on a Thursday then you're Phyllis any other time!" Thursday night, was usually a quiet night, so I arranged that I would take Linda to meet them, to Linda they were only voices on the phone, one of them, said to Linda, "Oh your Bill is ever so good to us, when I've had the operation he can break me in," and when I had to nip out on a call they said, "Go on, us girls will be alright all together" Anyway this relationship, for the want of a better word, ended when taking them home one night they started kissing each other, I warned them, but they decided to ignore me, so I threw the lot of them out in the middle of nowhere!

6th June 1975 I must have had a coach, as this was the date of a fatal train crash at Nuneaton, six people were killed, it had happened in the early hours of the morning, and work started straight away on clearing the track. I had an urgent phone call from the PMT asking if I could supply a bus to take a railway gang working overnight, it was a Friday and I remember it being hot. I did the job, getting to Nuneaton about 9 pm, parked up then I had to wait until 6 am, so I went to a local pub, thinking a pint will help me sleep, now I don't why but I always attract the village idiot, so I'm standing at the bar, when this guy starts making conversation, when he finds out that I'm on the train crash, this is what he said:

"You know I can't understand why people travel by train, I mean this train was the overnight train to Scotland, and you could catch a plane to Scotland, and I've seen these planes in the sky, they're only this size (holding his hand out) that's because they are that high up, and if they have a crash they have all that time to put parachutes on"

I thought it's safer to agree with him, he then asked me if I'd been into this other pub, I said "No why is it good?" his reply amused me, "Yes, but I'm banned," naturally I enquired why, he said "Because I have epileptic fits" I thought let's get out of here, and went back to the bus, got my sleeping bag out, got undressed and made my way to the back seat.

When I woke up, I realised my predicament, as I said before it was a hot night, and I've had a couple of pints. The back seat of a bus is not the most comfortable place to sleep, in my drink induced sleep, I had disposed with the sleeping bag, and I'm clad only in my underpants, with the rest of my clothes at the front of the bus. It was then that I realised where I had parked up, outside a block of high rise flats! It was like watching the sack race as I hopped down the bus and struggled to get dressed as onlookers walked past!
Stallington Hospital had now become a customer, they were having problems with staff transport, well, union problems, which resulted in strike's. They had their own buses for staff transport, after several meeting's I convinced them that I could offer a cost effective service, and went from being their preferred taxi operator, to taxi and bus operator.

Well everybody knew me; I was to one and all, Billy B Cabs! And if I was challenged by the picket's on the gate, I would tell them that I was collecting clock cards. In fact I was collecting blood samples from various wards, on this occasion it was Daffodil ward, (female wards were flowers, male wards were trees) as I walked in Sister was telling a patient off, "You are a naughty girl, Bill, isn't she a naughty girl?" I replied, "You are a naughty girl," I whispered to the Sister "What's she done?" the answer "She's just eaten the budgie!"

Linda was on a regular job taking a patients father to see his son Bertie on Birch Ward, there wasn't much choice between the two of them as who should have been a Mental patient. We would pick him up at his house in Lightwood, he would lock up, then stand there urinating against his own wall. Anyway as I've said Linda picked him up and took him directly to Birch Ward, as she was getting back into the car, she was approached by a patient, Billy Eckstein, (yes that's the correct name, and there was another patient called Sherlock Holmes) his words were "Woman fag" Linda said, "Sorry don't smoke," at that he tried to grab her, she managed to get into the car. He however tried to get at her through the open sunroof, failed and punched the boot of the car, leaving an indentation.

This was not the first time that we had problems with this patient, buts let's not forget he was a mental patient. On the other occasion, when we had a problem with him, it had involved one of my driver's, a new starter, I had warned him, that if a patient approaches you and says, "Man Fag", tell him to F off, this may seem harsh but it was the only thing he understood, and walk away, but he must have forgotten, Billy walked up to him, saying "Man Fag", my driver a very pleasant fellow said, "Sorry mate don't smoke" Billy ripped all the buttons off the front of his jacket! If my memory serves me right, the driver didn't stay with us long, anyway after the incident involving Linda on the Sunday, I decided to lodge a formal complaint, however the following day, Billy suffered a massive heart attack and died.

I had my fair share of characters amongst the drivers; let's start with Ron Watkins, who fancied a certain nurse, now Ron has since died, but the nurse I don't know about, so for the sake of this book we'll just call her Nurse. He eventually succeeded in arranging a date with her, Nurse was married, Ron wasn't, but what he had promised her was nobodies business. After the date, I asked Nurse how it went, she replied, "Bill he's an idiot, his idea of giving me a night out to remember, was a drive to the Arrivals Lounge at Manchester Airport watching the planes land!"

Drivers whenever possible were kept to the same bus, one day for some reason I had allocated Ron's bus to another driver, the bus was on a job out at Leek, Ron travelled to Leek, stormed up to the driver claiming that it was his bus, and started to remove his collection of CD music tape's, fair enough you might say, after all they were his. But he threw on them on to the road and stamped on them, ranting on about no else could play his music!

Staying with Ron, our depot at Tean also consisted of some dilapidated outbuildings, part of which was an old toilet block, no water or electric was connected to the buildings, and was not in use, well to any sane person, but then again were are talking about Ron. He used the toilet to empty his bowels, it was night time, he came out of the building pulling up his trousers as he came out of the darkness, unknown to him, he hadn't made sure his braces were clear of the pan, as he pulled his braces up, shall we politely say that his hands were somewhat contaminated!

Still with Ron, at a later date I had sacked him, he reported me to the Police for using a coach illegally. I had bought three Daimler coaches, and had them painted in identical liveries, the registrations being 305G, 306G & 308G, each vehicle had its own operators licence, and could not be used on any other vehicle. What I had done was, whilst a vehicle was off the road due to mechanical failure, I had changed the registration plates around, this was done to allow me to use another coach whilst I was a vehicle down, yes it was illegal, but only in my mind, a technicality. What Ron hadn't reckoned on was that I had a friend in the Police force, he called on me and informed me that my name had come up in the start of their shift briefing; there had been an accusation that I was using a coach without insurance or a MOT, was this true? I replied quite truthfully that the allegation was not true, my answer was truthful, it was insured!

I'm telling you this story because shortly after this Ron rang me up asking for a meeting which I agreed on, now bear in mind I'd sacked him, and he reported me to the police, what do you think he wanted me for? I couldn't believe it, he wanted me to go into partnership with him, breeding rabbits for export, naturally, I declined.

Roy Bagnall, was another one, known to one and all as Harry Worth, his wife had a somewhat dubious reputation, in fact when the Daimler Coaches arrived as they were painted into their liveries and they all carried Fleet Names, we had Tracy Karen, Keith Paul, and the last one Linda. Roy's wife was called Linda, he asked me if he could call his bus Linda, I told him that there wasn't enough space on the front for her name, he looked kind of puzzled and said, "but her name is the same as your wife's," I replied, "It's your wife that's called Slag Bag", he laughed and said "I'll tell her what you've said"

He came to work one day, and I passed comment about his tie, he said "Do you like it," I replied "Yes," he then went on to say, "I haven't bought it, Linda had been fooling around at the bus stop with some bloke, and took his tie off him, when I came downstairs this morning I found it back of the settee, he isn't getting it back" On another occasion Roy and I were on the 14.05 departure from Stallington, one went to Longton the other to Cheadle, we were sitting in the bus shelter when a female patient called Dorothy joined us, jokingly I said to her "Watch him, he's got three wives, six children, two white, one green, two blue & one yellow", she swiped him across the face, shouting "You dirty swine"

Then there was the time he rang me early one morning, to say that he had had a problem with his bus, the battery was flat, I said "Ok I'm on my way" Roy replied, "It's all right Bill I flagged a Lorry down and he's given me a snatch, but I've got another problem, well something's hanging down under the bus and is dragging along the road"

I replied "O.k. where are you, I'll get the mechanic out" Roy's response of "Well I haven't done my first trip yet on Stallington" panic stations, it appeared that he had fastened the tow rope around the power steering pump, there was a trail of oil from our depot to where he had stopped.

Before we leave Stallington Hospital let me tell you that they, or should I say the Hospital Management, would never have qualified as prompt payers, on one occasion besides my best effort's, their account got to be three months in arrears. So one day, I operated all the early morning journeys, then went to the Account Office at their head offices, and informed them the next scheduled journey was the 12.32 from Longton, but if they did not pay me at least for two months of the outstanding monies, then no more journeys would operate until such a time as they did. I also pointed out that the timetable was a registered service with the West Midlands Traffic area, and could operate only by the licence holder; I came away with a cheque.

Right lets talk about football, and staying with Roy, he had picked up a load of Stoke supporters from Blurton they were travelling to Sheffield. On his return to depot, he informed me that on the outward journey the bus had had a puncture "yep ok no problem", Roy then said "I didn't want to bother you, so I rang a tyre company up," "WHAT" I exploded, "Why what's up with the spare?" Roy smiled, and said "It hasn't got a spare wheel, I looked," at that I went to the bus lifted up the side locker and pointed at the spare wheel, Roy's response was "Oh I thought it was the same as a car, I looked in the boot."

As you can imagine I politely pointed out that the boot in coaches was where the luggage went! It cost more for the tyre than I got for the job, and it was only in Leek. Roy was not what you could describe as reliable on early morning timekeeping, Stallington Hospital required 2 buses at 6.30 every morning, Roy over slept quite often, I gave him a final warning, as I was sick and tired of knocking him up, the very next morning, no Roy, I needed him, so there I am again knocking him up again. Now if ever there was a competition for the best excuse for being late for work, quote this excuse: "Bill I'm sorry about this, but I'm deaf in one ear, so if I have to get up early, I have to sleep with my good ear up, and would you believe it but the wife must have turned me over in the night, as my deaf ear was up." Go on beat that for an excuse.

Another football job, I had bought an AEC Duple Continental coach, from Graham's, it was a cracker, it had a six speed gearbox and could out accelerate a car. Roy was thrilled that he was driving it, I can't remember where the destination was, I think it was Leeds, anyway Roy never said anything on the return, but I found later that passengers were not impressed with the coaches' performance. It transpired that Roy couldn't master the gearbox, so when the coach had to stop in traffic, the passengers had to pile off and run along side and jump back on as the coach picked up speed.

While we are on the subject of Football I'll tell you of a couple of my experiences, the first was relating to a coach journey to Norwich where Stoke were playing, this was the time when Stoke supporters had a bad reputation, and I could see why. I had had several requests for toilet stops, which I ignored, if I had stopped in a town they would have gone on a rampage. So in open countryside I pulled into a lay-by, thinking it was safe, wrong, they were exposing themselves to passing traffic and some of them went into a field throwing clods of earth at a tractor driver, and one of them even tried to get on the bus with a dead cat!

The other job strangely enough was in a similar area, this time Ipswich, it was the vehicle this time, not the passengers, the bus was a brand new Austin JU 250, twelve seater minibus, just out of the showroom. The minibus was a nightmare to keep in a straight line, if anything overtook you (and plenty did) the slip stream pulled you towards it, if you tried to overtake a lorry, as you drew level with it, the drag from the lorry pulled you not only towards it but held you there meaning you couldn't get past and when the lorry would pull away leaving you there, it wasn't the lorry driver it was my vehicle!

After I'd bought it, the Commercial Motor Magazine did a review on this model, it said "That the JU 250 cab is fitted as standard with a heater, the average driver will be that busy trying to keep it in a straight line, that he will have no need for it," the report was spot on, both my shoulders ached after that journey.

Then there was John Bailey, who had a chronic stutter, now he was a Walter Mitty character, talk about fib's he could spin a yarn. He came in one day late for his turn, to be fair this was unusual, when he did arrive I was out on his turn, when he came to relieve me I explained to him, that the coach, a Bristol RE, has a rather unusual gearbox, "No problem Bill I've driven these before, in fact I've driven all types," I said "Are you sure, because changing down from fifth into fourth, can be rather tricky," when I saw him later in the day, his shirt sleeve was torn in half, he'd done it trying to change gear! But it wasn't John's fault, it was the bus.

One day we were on hire to Copeland's Tours, travelling to London on a day trip for the Royal Doulton factory in Nile Street Burslem for their annual works outing, as you can imagine there were quite a few coaches, I think about eighteen in total, anyway, I had a couple of coaches on the job, and one was being driven by John. As the convoy made their way into the centre of London, in fact Edgware Road, the traffic was bumper to bumper and as John approached traffic lights they changed to Red. He carried on, but for only a few yards, as he was caught up in the traffic, as he sat there he could see in his mirror, that a mounted policeman was coming towards him, in John's word's; "He came galloping down, just like McCloud, (McCloud was a popular TV show at the time, based on the Royal Canadian Mounted Police) and if these buses don't move he's going to catch up with me," which of course he did.

The policeman knocked on his cab window, and ordered him off the bus, and to come to him, now don't forget John has a very bad stutter, "What's up" he stuttered, the Police Officer said, "You've just gone through those lights on red" the reply came "I didn't", at that the police horse moved, John shouted to the Police Officer "That bloody horse has just hit me," the officer ignored him, and again accused him of driving through a red light, this time John said, "Yes, but if I'd braked, all them other coaches would gone bang, bang in the back of me," the Police Officer asked him his name and age, he answered "John Bailey aged fifty two" Now to be fair to John he didn't look his age, his nickname was Danny LaRue, he had long silver hair, and always dressed young, like light blue jeans and a white polo neck top. Anyway the Police Officer didn't believe him, and repeated the question, "How old are you?" again the horse shifted position, John shouted out again "The bloody horse has hit me again," the Officer at that said, "Look I don't know where you are from, or how old you are, but get back into your bus, and remember that in London, red means stop!"

As seemed the norm with some of the drivers, he got himself involved with a female worker from Stallington, I don't now what led up to it, but he went off sick, claiming that he had cancer, he rang his female friend up and told her that he was at death's door, and because he lived on his own, he was being cared for by the Nun's.

I had become involved in another business, Robinsons Taxis in Stoke, I was in the office one day, when I heard an enquiry about if there any vacancy's for Taxi Driver's, I thought I'd know that stutter anywhere, yes, it was John Bailey. He couldn't see me so I let him talk awhile before making myself known to him. "Hello John, feeling better?" I enquired, he replied sounding very surprised "yes thank you," and then added "that he thought his sister had let me know that he wasn't coming back."

The next time I saw his female friend from Stallington, she told me of some of the tales he had told her, that he lived in a beautiful bungalow in May Bank, in fact it was a Prefab. He claimed that he had a son with no legs, a lie, he was divorced, a lie, under his bed he had box full of treasure, fantasy, and on their last meeting, he had come to say good bye as he had to go away for more intense cancer treatment, he had opened his treasure box, as he wanted her to have beautiful memories of their time spent together, so as she waved him goodbye with tears flowing down her cheeks, she opened her gifts, they were, wait for it, envelopes stuffed with Election Posters!

Let's tell you of another couple of amusing incidents at Stallington, Joe Lightfoot drove for me, at the hospital we had full use of the canteen facilities, but at weekends the opening hours were limited, so on Saturday's, in between runs we used the League of Friends facility. One of the patients on sighting Joe, got all excited, rushed over to Joe, showing him his new false teeth, the trouble was he had a mouthful of fruit cake and his teeth were coated in the cake.

Another time Joe had taken the patients off a female ward, on a two hour afternoon tour, on the return at the hospital, Joe being the gentleman, stood at the front holding the door open whilst they unloaded, remember these are mental patients, one of the patients took a shine to Joe, and grabbed him by his short and curlies! The nurse was trying to knock the patients hand away, saying let go, and poor Joe's hanging on for grim life.

The afternoon tours was a regular feature, basically to take the patients off the ward environment, these were operated on Monday's, Wednesday's and Thursday's. Tuesday's would see us taking them to the swimming baths at Shelton, this job was timed the same as the afternoon tours for a 4pm return, this enabled the bus to go on to its next job, which was taking the evening shift of cleaners into the Blythe Colours factory at Creswell.

Now remember they were mental patients, and were not averse to relieving themselves anywhere, on this job at Blythe Colours, there was one lady in particular who always dressed immaculately, on this occasion yours truly was driving, and as the ladies were getting off the coach at the colour works, I could see that she had sat on a wet seat, as the dye from the seat had run into her skirt, and where she had been wearing, a nice pink skirt, it was now sporting a large red circle! I didn't say anything to her, on the return journey she was waiting for me guns blazing, ranting on about having to sit in patients ***** (Urine) I replied that, "The bus hadn't been on hospital work, it had been on school baths, the children must have placed their wet towels on the seats," she calmed down on that news, (well I'd had time to think that one up), I bought her a box of chocolates and paid for the cleaning.

I knew which patient had wet the seat, as it had happened before, so what ever seat he chose to sit in, I would remove the upholstered seat cushion, and left him with the metal base to sit on, the strange thing was he would never wet on metal, only cloth.

The first coach I bought, was an old Ford Duple Yeoman, registered number 4799 RF, from Stevenson's. I engaged a sign writer to come and letter it up, in bold letters on the boot 'B.CABS TAXI SERVICES' then underneath equally bold letters 'LUXURY TRAVEL' it wasn't till I'd used the bus a few weeks that I found out that the sign writer couldn't spell, it actually read LUXERY, to rub it in when I sold the bus to McGuinesses for scrap, it sat on top of the pile, displaying the back end to the main road!

As the coach side took off, and we were getting busier by the day, we used to hire in other operators, one such operator was Jim Stonier. On this particular day his eldest son was the driver, he arrived at the hospital grounds, and as per our instructions, booked in at the telephone exchange, he then had to reverse up to the ward. As he started to reverse he was being helped by a male shouting "Come, come on, come on" bang straight into a brick wall, his helper was a mental patient!

We operated a School contract to the Glebe ESN unit (educationally sub-normal) at Fenton, this story centres around me taking them to the Shelton Baths, this was a Building housing a swimming bath for the disabled, and the water was always warm. I can't actually remember if it was room or body temperature, but as the teachers were all female

I used to help with the boys, I think there was only about two of them, and I would also swim with them. Well I did until the day I was swimming with my young charge, when I was aware of an object quite close to my nose, it was a turd! I can't recall volunteering again.

I had a Bedford Coach that had a faulty starter motor, if the motor stopped in one certain position it wouldn't start again. If you could move the starter motor, it would start; it would go for ages with no problem, then fail, anyway on this occasion it failed in the middle of Hanley, right outside Marks & Spencers. In those days you drove past there into Parliament Row, it was a Saturday afternoon, busy with shoppers, who all stopped and stared at the sight of a 53 seater coach, having a tow rope attached to a car, with the car towing the bus, it was on the level and it only had to move a yard, then it was O.K, but still a sight you don't normally see!

We also did work for a Cheadle travel agent, Terry Holmes, he specialised at the time in Maltese holidays. He was a walking disaster, what I didn't know, but soon found out, he couldn't understand the 24 hour clock. It was the Potter's holidays, and he had coaches from us taking holiday makers to both Manchester Airport and Gatwick Airport. On the return journeys on arrival at Manchester we found out that he had got the return times mixed up, we were there in fact 12 hours early, the people were still in Malta, so I rang him, pointing out his error, he apologised, agreed to pay the extra charges and I bought the buses back. Then as an after thought I checked the Gatwick flights, yes, he had done the same with them, so because of the distance, the drivers had to be accommodated in hotels, more about Terry Holmes later.

The day a driver reversed his bus into the brook trying to turn round in the depot situated at Blythe Bridge Rail station car park, was the day I decided to find another depot, that's how we ended up at St Thomas' Road, Tean. It was an open yard, with disused out-buildings, that at one time had housed toilets, plus an old building that was in a very bad state of repair, but there was room to park up my vehicles. The old building's we had tried to do something with it, so at least if it was raining we could work under cover on the minibuses, it was comical, at night we would try and make it secure, but when we came the next morning there would be a horse in it.

The horse belonged to a guy named Peter Sellars a well known Gypsy, (now Serving 10 years in gaol for drug dealing) we used to let it out, he would say that he'd got the right to put it there, and so it went on. Also on this site there was a Coach painting firm, called KDF. I did a deal with the owner, and dug out an inspection pit inside the building, the building was actually at the top of the yard, and situated at the top of a slight gradient, anyway I had it dug out, lined the walls with plastic sheeting, and then erected the walls using concrete blocks. It looked great and cost a few bob, it was forty foot long so that it could accommodate any of my coaches, but as I later found out, by talking to an old man of the village, Tean was riddled with underground streams, and we'd tapped into one. When we had a coach on the pit, first of all the pit had to be emptied, the water took a couple of hours to drain, and then even with the pump working it would still fill up!

One day I had a ministry man in doing a spot check, he wasn't best pleased waiting for the pit to empty, and then working in the pit with the water sloshing in, so as you may imagine he wasn't a happy bunny, especially as I took great delight in pointing out, that whilst he had been under my bus moaning about the conditions I expected him work under, there had been a thunderstorm, and he left his car window open.

Let me tell you about a couple of jobs involving Longton Police, one was mine, the other a fellow operator, Smallwood's Coaches. Firstly mine, a coach was hired by the C.I.D. for a men's night out in Blackpool, which to my knowledge at the time went without a hitch, it wasn't till years later that I found out in a chance conversation, that the driver had joined them on their visit to several clubs, which resulted in him getting drunk, and a Police Officer had driven the coach back!

Now to the other tale, Derek Smallwood rang me late one night, "Was I doing anything and had I had a drink," well I hadn't had a drink, it appeared that he had had this job taking a party to the Bass brewery, on the return journey the passengers had become concerned with the driver's driving, and complained to him, asking him if he had been drinking, his response? He took them to Longton Police Station asking the police to intervene, he was arrested for drink driving, and as Derek had had a drink could I nip down and return the passengers home, which of course I did. When he told me who the driver was, I wasn't surprised, as this guy had responded to an advert of mine for driver's, and came to see me under the influence of drink.

I had a coach stopped by the police for emitting excessive black smoke, both the driver and I received summons, the driver for driving the said vehicle, and myself as the owner, causing the vehicle to commit the offence. I decided to plead not guilty, and had to attend Fenton Magistrates Court, when the Magistrates entered the court, I was surprised to see that the chairman of the magistrates, George Stevenson, was known to me. I had previously worked with George at the PMT Fenton Garage, in fact he was the garage's union shop steward, he later went on to become a Member of Parliament, representing the Labour Party in Stoke on Trent, and then later became a member of the European Parliament.

Let's get back to the court case, I thought should I ask for an adjournment as we were known to each other, but then again, should he declare the fact, nothing from him, so I thought, well at least George had been a bus driver, and at least could understand the problem. How wrong could I have been, he fined me a hundred pounds which was the maximum, plus he also wanted to have my driving licence endorsed (with penalty points).

He wasn't best pleased when I challenged this, pointing out to the court, "That the offence is not endorsable" I said, the magistrates, plus the Clerk of the court went into a huddle, and then reluctantly informed me that I was correct. Afterwards even the two Police Officer's apologised to me on the severity of the fine, saying that "they went after the ones who could afford it". As a guide the case before me was a known criminal, he had 'death to pigs' tattooed on his fingers, was charged with criminal damage to a police car. He had in fact thrown a bottle at it, his sentence was a misery fine of £10. I can tell you that after the case, I never spoke to George again, and certainly never voted for him!

At that time we had a static caravan at Alton Towers, which we as a family enjoyed at weekends, for some reason this weekend we hadn't got the children with us. A friend and fellow operator David Cheadle and his girl friend, Gillian, had come to visit us, this was way before it became a theme park, but it did have its own pub within the grounds called the Ingestre Arms, these were the times when I enjoyed a drink or two or maybe three or even four.

So David and I, were having a drinking session, Linda and Gillian were with us, but they took a more sensible approach, we even got the site maintenance man, Eddy, drunk, More of him after. I said to David, "you'd better stop the night", "can't" was the reply, "Why," I asked, "Gillian hasn't brought her birth pills with her," "no problem says I", as I went round the pub, asking people if anyone could lend them a birth pill, no success, then still "can't", " why" I again asked, "I'm on Drake Hall Prison contract tomorrow, taking the prisoners to Church", again "No problem mate, I'll get you up". I set my alarm for 7.30 a.m., off it went, I stopped it and went back to sleep, Linda's shaking me saying, "What about David," I said, "Stuff Cheadle", and went back to sleep.

As Linda and I had the bedroom, they had had to sleep head to head on the seating area, and every time he thought he would climb off and visit Gillian, or go to the toilet, our dog,

Shandy would growl at him. The coach contract at Drake Hall Woman's Prison, he lost for being unreliable! Guess who got it? Yep me! Talking about Drake Hall, it was Christmas Day, and the prisoner's had to go to church. It was freezing weather I arrived at the prison in time, but couldn't open the doors to the coach; the air tank had frozen up. I borrowed a pair of step's so that they could board the bus via the emergency door, and I waited and waited, eventually the officer in charge came out apologising, but added a comment that it was my fault. Apparently one of the prisoners had recognized me, and was refusing to board the bus, it was years later that I found out who it was, it was a female taxi driver from the Potteries who had been convicted of informing burglars of empty houses, she had in fact taken the residents to the airports!

Ah yes, Eddy, the maintenance manager at Alton Towers, well not long after this, he came after my blood, he claimed that due to David and I getting him drunk he'd gone home and got his wife pregnant!

I bought a double decker, I rang the insurance broker up and never thought any more about it. I did a deal with KDF coach painters who painted it for free, in exchange for an advert on the exterior, and Millmoor bodies re-panelled it, again, no charge for an advert in the interior. I used it a couple of times then was told that the brokers were not able to obtain insurance cover required due to Stoke on Trent having a large number of bridges, so it was sold!

Back to the Taxi side, we had a Special School contract taking children to a school in Leek, the first pick up was in Blythe Bridge which was a young Downs Syndrome girl, who had severe learning difficulties. Her favourite game was I-Spy, the one that comes to mind was "I spy with my likkle eye something being with B, after about half an hour we gave up, the answer, Purple. The second pick up was another young girl from a farm in Dilhorne, she was wheelchair bound, and had to be man handled into the car, the problem was at the location, was that they had two Alsatian dogs, who were no problem whilst you were stationary, but the minute you drove away they attacked the tyres, on at least two occasions they bit through the walls of the tyres! I tried to get the farmer to secure the dogs, he wouldn't or couldn't, so I refused to travel into the actual farm, and they had to bring the girl to the road to meet our car, not really a satisfactory answer.

Brian Heaton was working with us at this time, and I did a deal with him, at 6pm in the evening I had a switch by the side of our telephone, and hey presto our number 3898 became 5409 ex directory, BT were clever even in those days, and Brian's home number became 3898, but this wasn't really what I was looking for, as it was at that stage that the business ran me, not as it should be, me running the business.

So, when I was approached by Peter Robinson of Robinson Taxis, the deal he offered me was that I could run the coaches from an office in their taxi base in the centre of Stoke, giving 24 hour telephone coverage; in return I would merge my taxis with his fleet. He and his wife Joy, would run the taxis and would share in the profits, it seemed too good to be true, as it proved out to be. I gave my full attention to the coach side and left the taxis to him, changing my trading name for the coach side to B.C. Travel, same initials as B Cabs Taxis, but now it stood for Better Class Travel. Before we leave here I'll tell you about a gimmick I came up with for a name change this was some time before, I told the drivers I'd had a brainwave and what did they think about changing the name from B.Cabs to using my initials Thomas William Stanton's Associated Taxi Services, it was only a joke, but it certainly caused a few comments, I'll leave it to you to come up with your interpretation.

Robinson's fleet of cars left a lot to be desired, but with my input of cars and fresh investment in the way of Hire Purchase against six new cars, Lada's, though after six hundred miles the tyres were as smooth as a baby's bottom, apparently they were supplied with Russian tyres that were not suitable for

British roads. We then bought six new Peugeots, all seemed well, then just after a year Peter dropped dead, he was dining out at about midnight and suffered a massive heart attack, by 6am the following morning I was getting frantic phone calls from worried creditors, unknown to me he had been systemically creaming off cash, they, (him and his wife,) had bought a holiday bungalow at Talacre Beach, in Wales not a caravan, a brick built bungalow!

Now we as the four directors of Robinsons had stood as joint and several guarantors, on the hire purchase of the six new Peugeot cars, the four being myself and Linda, Peter and Joy.

The cars were made the subject of a repossession order, Joy would not agree to the signed agreement, saying that she was only liable to pay a quarter because Peter had died, the finance company General Guarantee took me to court because in their view, and correctly so, they would go after the best option available to recoup the money, which was something like fifteen thousand pounds. In court their area manager, who was and is still a friend of mine, introduced me to their solicitor, Mr Woolliscroft, all the facts were explained to him, with the rider added that I was in fact a friend. Mr Woolliscroft looked me in the eye, and said "Mr Stanton my instructions today are to kick you in the balls, and I will do so" and he did, but you have to admire his honesty and straight forwardness. To meet this demand I had to sell my prized possessions, two new coaches, and settle for two older one's I had taken in part exchange, more about that later.

Staying with the Robinsons saga I had an allegation that a lady had just got out of one of our taxis, and the driver was drunk, not only that, he was sat outside her house drinking out of a bottle. I called him several times on his car two way radio, which he ignored, the last being that I had been made aware that he was drunk, and if he didn't respond I would call the police, he didn't, I did. The Police arrived and breathalysed him, this would have been in 1976 and the breathalyser was in its infancy, he passed it! Yet he couldn't stand up!   All he could say/slurred was "Thank you you've proved me innocent!" Innocent or not he was sacked.

Talking to another Police Officer about this at a later date, he said the Police Officer involved was a rookie, and should not have let him smoke his pipe, and because of the state he was in he should have insisted on a blood test.

Job No 32, Not So Nu Kar Rentals

As an offshoot I started a new business it was a car hire business based on an American idea, Rent a Wreck, hence the name Not So Nu Kar Rentals and it really took off. The coaches were based at Tean and my offices were in Stoke, so the cars were located at Stoke. I think I had about fifteen cars.

The average price I paid for each car was about fifty pounds and they were rented out at thirty five pound's plus VAT per week, and we were busy, the trouble was the idea was for the punters to hire them for local use only, but we used to get enquires asking if they could take them abroad! I used to say you'll be lucky if they got you to the docks! Mondays morning's quite often the AA recovery trucks were in a line waiting to unload.

An assistant manager at Barclay's Bank, Stoke, hired a Vauxhall Viva, to go to Sunderland, when he bought it back I asked him, "How's it gone?", he said "Well on the motorway it wanders at speed" "That's cross-ply tyres" was the answer. He then said that "The wipers lifted off the screen," my reply, "Cross winds", "and the rear bumper was tied up with string", now I knew that this comment wasn't true, as it was my boot laces! So after he'd finished moaning I said to him; "Just think if the car had been perfect all you could have said was, thank you and here's the keys, instead here we are having an intelligent conversation," exit one assistant bank manager.

I had one woman complaining that the car had a flat battery; she wasn't amused with the answer that it was square when she took it out. On another occasion I had a car returned from a two week hire, the female hirer, thanked us but said that the brakes required adjusting. I explained to her that the car, a Ford Capri, had recently had a new engine fitted and that it was company policy to leave brakes requiring adjustment so that the hirer's would drive slowly. She agreed saying "Do you know you're right I've driven ever so carefully because of the brakes". I wouldn't have been so flippant had I have known that the car was hired by Social Services for surveillance work!

Another car, an Austin 1100 (which the majority were) had been on hire for eight weeks to an American lady, when the car was returned you couldn't see the dashboard for parking tickets! All were unpaid! (but not my responsibility). Another 1100 when we managed to find it, was being used as a chicken shed!

The Ford Capri, went out on hire and was never returned, I eventually tracked it down to a car breakers yard. The hirer claimed that he had returned the car, but as no one was there at the time, he had put the keys through our letter box, and I couldn't prove any different.

I remember the time I'd had to hide around the corner, after I've hired the last car out, the indicator stalk on a Volvo 144 had broke, so I'd stuck it in position, then vanished. Another Volvo this time a 164 broke down in Cornwall, and came back via AA relay, the hirer came in the office asking for a refund; I asked him (knowing the answer) "When did it break down?"

"Friday" was the answer, "And how much petrol did you use to get back?" "Obviously none," "There's your refund" said I.

To assist in my many vehicle purchases I bought myself a Ford Transit pickup truck that had been converted to a Recovery Truck, and as such was exempt from the MOT testing system. It was a mean beast and had a 3 litre V6 Petrol engine, and as the saying goes, it could pull a house down! Anyway one of the nurses at Stallington approached me enquiring if her son, Bill Hancock, could borrow it. He'd just joined the RAF and was stationed at RAF Cranford, which is just the other side of Grantham, and needed to get his car back. I agreed but pointed out that vehicle had to be used using Trade Plates, and for insurances purposes could only be used by employees, so if he was stopped he would have to say he was employed by B.Cabs.

Well as you can guess he was stopped on a Ministry of Transport check point, and although the vehicle was MOT exempt, it had to be roadworthy. Again as you have guessed faults were found, and the vehicle had to taken off the road with immediate effect, acting on the Polices instructions it was parked up in a nearby lay-by to await collection or repair. The driver was cautioned and all details were taken, including mine. The following day I accompanied by my mechanic travelled out to recover the vehicle, guess what? It had been stolen; and I never saw the vehicle again!

Then to add insult to injury I was summoned to appear at Bingham Magistrates Court, for causing the said vehicle to be used with defective parts, they did consider charging me with using it without insurance, as the terms of the policy stated employees only. But as I pointed out it also included casual drivers. I also stated that the driver had since this offence joined the Army, this simple mistake gave him time to settle into the RAF routine, eventually they did catch up with him and he was summoned and fined for his part. Apparently it is well known fact that the Police have a saying relating to the use of trade plates, 'red and white, stop on sight!'

It was about this time when I had visit from a VAT officer called Mr Simister. I had tried to defraud the Customs and Excise, remember me having to sell my two new coaches, it so happened at the time of the sale, the Customs and Excise (VAT) were on strike, my business were classed as a VAT Zero rated business. This meant that the VAT, I had paid out on my purchases on fuel etc was refunded on a monthly basis, the VAT actually owed me about six thousand pounds. By not declaring the sale of two coaches and the part exchanges I thought they wouldn't tie it up, as the sale had been in Peterhead in Scotland, but I was wrong, I was cautioned and informed of my rights. He went on to explain the VAT officers had more power than the Police, and if decided at head office, an offer could be made 'To compound the proceedings' by paying a penalty, it wouldn't go any further other than paying a penalty I wouldn't have a criminal record, would I be interested if it was offered, I agreed saying, "That at least it wouldn't have to go through the courts", meaning no publicity, he went away for further advice, a couple of weeks later, he was back.

"Mr Stanton, I told Head office that you were a reasonable man, and that you had agreed with the charges and that you were willing to pay a penalty, they have agreed to this request and set the sum of three thousand pound's to keep this out of court." Now this was the exact amount that I was charged in defrauding them, I replied, "This in my opinion is blackmail, no disrespect to yourself, but tell them to get stuffed" he replied, "I understand your frustration, and sympathize with you" The very next day, he rang the Office, and spoke to Linda, saying "You know Mrs Stanton, your husband is a very foolish man, he could still be fined three thousand pounds and get sent to prison." This of course worried Linda, but she could only say "Well you know what's he's like."

So, I took my chance in court, I was summoned to appear at Fenton Magistrates Court, 2pm on a Friday. I thought this can't be bad, no publicity it will be too late to appear in the

Evening Sentinel, and I was right, nothing in the press. I was charged with two offences of trying to defraud Her Majesty's Customs and Excise, one for each coach, remember VAT wanted me to pay three thousand pounds, I was fined thirty pounds on each charge, as we came out of court Mr Simister said, "You were lucky there Sunshine!" I replied "Yes and two thousand nine hundred and forty pound's better off," but of course it carried a criminal conviction.

Back to B.C. Travel and coaching, one of my customers was Newcastle OAP's. I would take them on a week's holiday usually in early May, then once a month on a day trip. On arrival at our chosen destination for the holiday, I always followed the same procedure, arrive Saturday, day off Sunday, Monday half day tour, Tuesday full day, Wednesday & Thursday half day's, Friday off and Saturday return. On this particular occasion I'm not sure of the destination, but I think it was Paignton. In the evening's I would stay with them in the hotel and either mix with different groups staying in the hotel or call Bingo. If I fancied a drink or go out with another coach driver, it would be after 9.30 pm. as I've said Sunday, day off, well it wasn't really a day off. I would wander around the resort, looking at coach operators window display's or advertising board's, finding out what was suitable for my party, then visiting places such as the Tourist Information centre's, finding out as much as I could about the area's I had in mind to visit.

After telling you all this you'll find out it's nothing to do with the story, anyhow, this was later in the week, I'd called Bingo, had a chat with some of them etc., and said my goodnights. I'd only been in the bedroom a few minutes, when there was someone knocking at the door, I opened the door, and lo and behold I've got a pensioner trying to kiss me and force her way into my bedroom, I said something like, "Don't be silly," and shut the door, amused and slightly scared to tell the truth. The next morning nothing was said, so I acted normally, but did ask discrete questions about her, she was a widow in her eighty's and one assumes lonely. I felt sorry for her, and talked to her as if nothing had happened, after the holiday I next took them out at the beginning of June, this was on a daytrip to Chester. It was on this daytrip that she gave me a parcel and card for my birthday, I thanked her pointing out that it was some three weeks away. On the return journey we stopped at a pub, she sat down on a stool and leaned back, forgetting that it was a stool, causing her to fall onto the floor, she was picked up and we all had a laugh not only at her, but with her. I dropped them off at night at various locations around the Newcastle area, and that night she died in her sleep.

When my birthday arrived I opened the card and present, it was a wallet and she had placed a lucky silver horseshoe in it, on the card she thanked for me for a wonderful holiday, now you know all the facts, consider this, she has died, and within a very short period of time I was bankrupt, I kept the wallet and threw the charm away!

On my return journey from being away with the Newcastle pensioners I would arrange with Linda to meet me somewhere close to home, like Trentham Gardens. Linda would bring Tina with her, and leave her with me for the drop off's, the passenger's would give Tina gift's of money, (my collection), she thought it was great. On one occasion Linda and Tina came with me on a holiday to Tenby, and a fantastic time was had by all, the most memorable moment was Tina making her way across the dance floor, with her Ladybird book of hymns and addressing Bob the pianist saying, "Bob, if you can play this tune, I'll sing it."

One day I had a phone call from a guy I'd met in Bournemouth, at the time he was the assistant manager at a hotel I'd stayed in, his name was Eddy. I'd forgotten all about him, until he rang me up, he explained that he was now the manager at the Queen's Hotel, Blackpool, he had been hired to start doing cabaret break's, similar to what he had been doing in Bournemouth, and was I was interested in promoting the Queen's? After meeting him and the Hotel's owner's I decided to try it, we agreed that if we both used the same parallels in pricing, cheap and cheerful, it should do well.

Well it did amazing business, we did one weekend break per month, from the end of the Illumination's till the beginning of May, cabaret weekend's, full board, Friday evening meal through till Sunday returning after Lunch, plus five day breaks half board Monday through to Friday. We had waiting lists for availabilities, in fact one year I did an Easter five day break, and filled the hotel, I had four coaches full, never again did I try to do anything as ambitious, they all wanted sea views and they wanted the same rooms as when they were on the weekend breaks, we just couldn't accommodate all their wishes.

When I say we had waiting lists, how my system worked, was that I reserved enough room's to fill my coach, when this was full, I would have from the hotel a list of other room's available and sell them to any interested parties who had their own transport, but they still had to pay the same as everyone else. Brilliant, people were travelling from as far as Nottingham and Birmingham. When my eldest daughter, Tracy got married she enjoyed a five day stay as a wedding present from the Hotel's management. Still at the Queen's and as a coincidence it was on Tracy's birthday, Linda and I were invited as the hotel's guests to the grand reopening of the Cabaret bar. We were sitting in the VIP area, enjoying the night's entertainment, unfortunately though the sound system broke down. The entertainment that night consisted of about twelve different artist's, however, without the sound system they could not be heard in the VIP area, so the choice was, stay where you were and although you could not hear the cabaret, the hospitality was free, or join the crowd, enjoy your self but pay.

Surprise, surprise we stayed put, and made acquaintance with our table companion's, Rudy and Pat Mancini, who owned the Palm Court Hotel, it was not their intention at the time, but later on they actually became the new owners of the Queen's, so we didn't need any introductions. Rudy was a very talented musician in fact he claimed that he was related to Henry Mancini. Sadly, Rudy died of cancer after taking over The Queens Hotel meaning that Pat was still in charge as sole proprietor (she died in 2010).

After I'd finished as a coach operator, I introduced Mike and Pam Burn, of Copeland's Tours, for them to carry on with this very successful venture, a meeting had been arranged, followed by a complementary lunch at the hotel.
We were in the company of the hotel's general manager, Joe, (note the manager is now Joe, Eddy had long gone, fingers in the till) Pat Mancini recognized Linda and I, and came over to

our table, of course I introduced her to the Burns. Mike trying to be clever and a heavy hint of sarcasm, said to Pat, "You're nothing like Bill described you," Pat of course turned to me and asked, "How did you describe me," I said, "Common as muck and as hard as nails," Pat smiled and said, "Bill's got me to a T." the comment had backfired on him.

On one of the cabaret weekends, some of my regular guests had previously been in conversation with one of the hotels chefs, and had been telling him about Oatcakes, he told them the next time that they came to bring some with them, so lo and behold two dozen were given to the chef for the Sunday morning breakfast, they had explained to him that we eat them with Bacon, Sausage and Egg. Come the Sunday morning the breakfast was served, as a full English Breakfast, accompanied with Oatcakes stuffed with all the fillings as well.

The Queens was another venue where Tina was in her element, often joining the compere and singing, The Blackpool Belle, even now twenty odd years later, she still knows the words.

Back with Mike Burn, I was in his office one day when news came in that one of my coaches had been involved in a head on collision with a PMT coach, I immediately shot off, accompanied by Mike. The accident had occurred on a country road at a place called Ellastone, my coach was travelling empty to Mayfield to collect school children whilst the PMT was en-route from Mayfield to Uttoxeter and had approximately forty children on board; all suffering injuries of various degrees, although none were serious, thank God.

The road had been closed, and by the time I had explained my reason's to access the area, the recovery vehicle's were in position and the children had been taken away in a fleet of ambulances. My coach had taken the brunt of the vehicle damage. On the point of impact, the PMT coach had collided with a pole carrying overhead wires, Mike immediately took charge of the recovery and climbed onto the tow bar of the PMT recovery truck, as he did so, he steadied himself by holding onto the offending pole, wow, it was live! That made him jump!

My coach was a write off, my driver, Ron Powell, had no injuries except to his pride. The accident had completely flattened the front of my vehicle, so to get out, he had to jump out of the emergency door, unfortunately his jacket collar had got caught on the hinges, so he had to be rescued by the fire-fighter's, he did have a few cuts around his knees caused by broken glass, but nothing major. I called at his house that night to see him (and strangely enough I saw him to talk to recently, and he reminded me of this conversation on that night), I went to comfort him and reassure him, in return I was getting comments about his recently purchased jeans, and I do remember saying to him, "Are you trying to claim for a new pair of jeans from me?" He confirmed this, so in return I asked him, "Am I asking you to pay for the damage caused to my bus?" End of conversation! To be fair to my driver Ron, who was subsequently fined for driving without due care and attention, the roads were very icy and slippery.

It has to be said, that I did have a lot of attention from the Ministry relating to maintenance of my vehicle's, or should I say, lack of. I did employ fitters, but the conditions they were expected to work under was shall we say, poor, but I tried to keep on the right side of the law, but often failing, which resulted in me being a regular visitor at the Traffic Commissioners in Birmingham. Now I must be honest although the Ministry hounded me, they never fabricated any defects, but I did have a competitor who certainly didn't help matters. He would constantly inform the Ministry of my misdemeanours, I do know that some, not all, of the Ministry inspectors felt sorry for me, buts that's life.

Some of the problems were of my own doing, for instance, I had a friend at Rugeley, a fellow operator, who had a coach involved in an accident where a Police Officer had been fatally injured, his licences were suspended, and I lent him one of my coaches complete with an operator's license. I was prosecuted for allowing a vehicle to be driven without insurance, now you are probably thinking no insurance, serves me right, but in fact the coach was insured by me, and insured by my friend, but the ruling was, because he was operating without his operators licence, that made his and mine insurance null and void, I made no personal gain, I was only trying to help a friend.

Another instance was the time I had use of the facilities at Longton Transport, when I say facilities I mean use of their outside inspection pit. I'd had yet another spot inspection of my vehicles, this time it was a twenty nine seater Bedford coach, which had a broken rear spring. We were aware of this and had placed an order for a new one, but they hadn't got one in stock. They could have refurbished the existing spring but that would have meant the coach being off the road, but I hadn't got a replacement vehicle. So on my instructions, we codged it by securing a piece of wood into position, covering the wood with dirt so that hopefully it would pass at a glance, but I knew that it would not pass the examiners inspection, so I told the driver to take it to Longton Transport, and draw onto the pit for a front end inspection only.

After this initial examination, I knew that the examiner will tell me to instruct me to turn around and reverse onto the pit, when this happened you reverse off and then make your way for the job you are on, under no circumstances take any notice of what I, or any else says, result, myself and the examiner jumping up and down at the stupidity of the driver misunderstanding simple instructions, result, or should I say, relief, that's one I got away with, the spring was on the next day.

I got myself into more trouble over some tyres, I held an account with Motorway Tyres, their rep offered me a deal of a huge discount on a tyre, it was an unknown name brand to me, however he assured me that it was a leading name manufacturer, using the name 'Henley'. The difference in price of about Seventy pound's, it was a one off, and there was only one available at this price; so I quite naturally bought it. It was an 1100 size, which fitted a couple of my coaches, I also used 900 sizes. Shortly after, I had a visit from their tyre fitter, Mick Quigley, offering me a good deal on 900's, and I could have six of them. I thought this is too good to be true, the problem being that I had to put the cash up front, which I did. He delivered the tyres, but on delivery they were Michelin, it was obvious they were knocked off, but what do I do, he's had my cash, and I've got the tyres. I duly received an invoice for the full amount, I approached the fitter, he assured me it was no problem, a credit note would follow, but it didn't and I then started received invoices for tyres I hadn't received.

I rang up Motorway Tyres and was informed that he was off sick, I thought this is blackmail, he thinks I can't do anything because I've received stolen tyres, so I went to the Police, made statement's, not telling the police the truth about my involvement with the original tyres. He was arrested and I was taken in for questioning, of course I denied having an illegal involvement, the tyres in question, I had hidden them away at my friend's yard in Rugeley, in short giving the police the run around.

Eventually a warrant was issued for my arrest, but I was on a caravan holiday in Cornwall, I was told to report to Longton Police Station as soon as I returned, which I did. Well, the following day, as soon as I entered the Police station I was cautioned and handcuffed, but I knew without the evidence they hadn't got a case, they put me in a cell, and left me there, thinking they would frighten me, no lunch, just me in a cell. I heard my name mentioned, Mr Stanton, "Yes he is under arrest and being held here, no, you can't speak with him," apparently I had a minibus in trouble in Birmingham and Linda was asking to speak to me asking if the vehicle carried a spare fan belt.

The female police sergeant rather grudgingly relayed the message, and I was able to confirm that the vehicle did indeed have a spare, it was under the drivers seat, (remember the Police woman for later). Anyway unknown to me the Police bought one of my drivers into the cell area, asking if they recognised my shoes outside the cell door. He didn't fall for it, but then they brought my traffic manager in, he said "Yes" they then threatened him his shoes would be joining mine, so he told them everything.

I eventually went to court on the 30th November 1979 on two charges of handling stolen goods and I was fined two hundred and fifty pound's on each charge, the other guy was fined the same amount, but he was also ordered to do so many hours community work. (I can tell you the dates because it is on my CRB disclosure).

Now remember the Police woman, well some time later, Linda and I were invited to a charity race night, it was held at Blythe Bridge High School, as we entered, the female publican from the Butchers Arms, Forsbrook, called us over, "Here you are Bill, I've saved you a couple of seats," bet you've guessed that her companion was the one and only Police sergeant! Now tact has never been one of my better points, and I took delight in embarrassing the woman with my recollection of the time I was her prisoner! I don't think she stopped long!

In the 1970's all P.S.V's (Public Service Vehicles) were every seven years subject to having the vehicle's C.O.F. (Certificate of Fitness) renewed, it was very strict, I took one of the recently purchased Daimler Roadliners, to the PMT's Stoke garage for the C.O.F. test. I'm in the cab, listening for the shouted instructions, like apply your brakes, turn the steering wheel etc., I could hear the vehicle examiner talking to his assistant, about how he liked these Plaxton bodies, I thought magic, imagine my surprise when at the end of the test, he presented me with three pages of defects.

Talking about these Daimler's, they were powered by a Perkins V8 engine, situated at the rear, a massive lump of metal, at times they wouldn't turn off and you couldn't stall them, as they were semi-automatics (no clutch). The only way to stop the engine was to cover the air intakes. I'd seen how my mechanic did it, he opened the boot lid, which gave you a clear view of the engine, he then put his hand over the air intake, and hey presto the engine would stop.

On this occasion, firstly, I was in the pub and it was either late at night or early in the morning, when I received a call that the driver returning from a trip was at the depot and couldn't turn the engine off, no problem I'll will be with you in a few minutes. Don't forget I thought I knew how to do it, except my hands compared to the mechanics were like fairies, the engine nearly sucked me in, it sobered me up, I had to get a seat base and put it over the air intake.

Another job I used to do on a regular basis, was taking the residents of a couple of Old Folk's Home's out for a short trip, I did Mill Hill, Abbey House and Eardley House. The two that come to mind both involve Eardley House, the first one was I had taken them, by them, I mean the residents and the staff, on an afternoon tour around the Peak district, and as was always the case, stopping for alcohol consumption at a friendly pub. On this trip after the pub stop, I made my way to the home of Eardley House's hairdresser, Michael, who if I describe as being feminine, I think I'm being more than fair. Anyway, his house was situated just before Hartington's lake. I pulled up outside the property; on the outside it appeared to be a mid terraced house, with beautiful front gardens. I remember it being a beautiful summer's day; the resident's stayed on the coach, whilst the majority of the staff went into the house.

As was often the case I had to chase the staff for a departure, I made my way into the kitchen of the house, and couldn't believe my eyes, as you can imagine with alcohol being involved, there was plenty of noise and laughter, and the cause of the laughter was centred on the upstairs landing, now, you must realise that I was known to all the staff, and again it's fair to say that I had a reputation as being game for a laugh.

They were urging me to go to the toilet upstairs, so off I went upstairs, and this is where I couldn't believe my eyes, the toilet was situated in the middle of the enlarged landing! You could sit on the pan and hold a conversation with anyone in the kitchen, my comments of, "What an original idea to keep flies out the kitchen" was greeted with lots of laughter.

The other job was an evening tour, a couple of hours travelling around the countryside, and then stopping off at a country pub. On this occasion I took them to the Roebuck in Forsbrook, again a good time was had by all. In the pub some members of staff had met with one of Forsbrook's characters, and purchased sacks of potatoes, I loaded them into the boot of the coach, however, on arrival at Eardley House, the sacks were half empty and the boot had loads of potatoes lying around. I collected them up and re-bagged them, but on the invoice I worded it as; 'For the hire of a coach travelling from Eardley House, for an afternoon tour around the Buxton area, plus the collection of six tons of bagged potatoes,' Matron didn't read it properly and passed the invoice to Staffs County Council for payment, and it was paid.

I've mentioned before a fellow operator who caused me trouble, here are a couple of examples; during the night I had a couple of coaches vandalised, several windows had been broken including the windscreen in one, the side windows were replaced by a Glass firm, the windscreen however was a different story. I eventually through Lawton Body Repairs, located one, the problem was it was at the Plaxton factory in Scarborough. I had just bought a new Peugeot 504 family estate car for use as a Taxi, and as such it was taxed and insured for business use, so to me this was the logical choice of vehicle, it was new and had the room for the carriage of a bus window screen.

As I approached Scarborough I noticed a hitchhiker, my attention was drawn to the fact that he had Trade Plates with the then Staffordshire Registration, RF. I collected the screen, and immediately returned home. On the outskirts of Scarborough I came across the hitchhiker still thumbing a lift, so I stopped and picked him up, it transpired that he was from Tipton and had delivered a Reliant Robin Three Wheeler. As soon as we hit the A1 the Police stopped me, they were obviously waiting for me, as soon as I stopped the Police went and checked my Road Fund licence, which was classed as Hackney, this meant it could only be used for the carriage of passengers.

Now I've always had the ability to think on my feet, so I got out of the car, and asked what the problem was? They of course stated the obvious, "Why was I using a car for business use" to which I replied "It's a Taxi, and I've been to Scarborough to collect this Gentleman, and this was his luggage" by the look on the Police Officers face, I think he was relieved at my answer, this in my opinion was because no one likes being used. But what a dirty trick to pull; talk about kicking a man when he's down, two coaches vandalised and then this!

Another time on the Stallington Hospital Staff contract, we operated every day expect on a Sunday with two buses, but on a Sunday morning only, I had to find an extra vehicle to cover the Bentilee area, there was never any need other than a car, so Linda would do this. Tracy had just passed her driving test, so she volunteered to do this, so that her Mum could have a lie in, as she approached each pick up point, she was confronted by this person (person is not the word I'm looking for, but not lets swear), he would draw up to her in his car and take a photo, this tactic was obviously upsetting and intimidating especially for a seventeen year old girl.

He complained to the ministry that I was using an eight seater minibus and a six seater Peugeot car illegally, it should be noted that after I had ceased trading, he used his Peugeot car on the same type of work. The Ministry's view of my use of these vehicles was that it was a grey area of the law, and could not be enforced. Then again feeding the Ministry of my wrong doings, he informed them I was using a bus with worn tyres, when the Ministry called on me, they must have passed the tyre fitters on their way home.

I was aware of who was making these allegations against me, as some but not all, were sympathetic and I knew that they were being used as a tool against me. The strange thing about it all, he himself could not see anything wrong in the amount of hassle he was causing, in his mind it was a normal business tactic, as was demonstrated by the following story.

It happened on a Sunday morning, the ill feeling between ourselves was at its height, when he telephoned me to say that I would be pleased to know that he just had an accident, and was waiting for an ambulance. I naturally enquired about the incident, although admittedly it was through gritted teeth, he went on to say, "That I would pleased to know that he had fallen off the depot roof,"
I replied asking him as to the extent of his injuries, apparently he had broken his ankle, on hearing this, I told him, "Thanks for letting me know, its Sunday today, but tomorrow morning, I'm going back to the shop, where I purchased the voodoo doll from, and ask for my money back", he replied "Why its worked hasn't it" my return comment was "Is your neck ok," end of conversation.

Years later on his first heart attack, I visited him in hospital, well life's too short to hold grudges, but it didn't stop me from saying to him from his hospital bed, "Bloody hell, you haven't far to go, the morgue is more or less opposite". There are a couple of sayings, one is 'What goes around, comes around' and the other is, 'Evil be to him who Evil thinks,' and the older you get the more you realise that its true, I often think about these sayings, as I live a comparatively pain free life, against his life stuck in wheelchair.

Before we leave B.C. Travel, I'll tell you a story that was told to me by a fellow coach driver, personally I don't believe it, but here goes. I was on an eight day tour somewhere down south, and there was a group of drivers talking, when the subject got round to passengers dying, I knew, but you may not know, that for every county border a dead body is carried over, a fee has to be paid to the relevant authority. Now we come to the story, this driver swore it was true, as he claimed that he personally knew the people involved. This family had gone on a camping holiday, abroad, and had taken Granny with them. Unfortunately Granny died, and it was going to cost a fortune to bring her back, so they wrapped Granny up in the tent, put it on the roof rack and returned home. When they drove off the ferry, someone had stolen the tent, and they have never seen Granny or the tent since! As I've said, I'm a non believer, you can please yourselves, just imagine opening the tent, wow this ones got a Totem pole!

As I mentioned before I had to sell my two new vehicles to raise funds to pay the debts incurred with Robinson's Taxis, and I never really got over the financial problems, leading to me being declared Bankrupt in 1986. In case you're wondering what happened to Not So Nu Kar Rentals, as I mentioned before how busy we were, so being acutely aware that I needed money, across the road from my office in Stoke, there were two brothers operating a car sales business, so when people enquired about hiring a car, I would direct them to their car sales; they in turn would send them up to us.

The younger brother Brian would use our toilets, and I would engage him in conversation, I would thank him for sending these people to us, and point out that we couldn't cope with influx of fresh business. It wasn't long before Brian had convinced his elder brother to buy the business from me, they renamed it Magnum, the elder brothers name? John Cauldwell, who is now a billionaire, and is probably Stoke on Trent's richest man! But I hasten to add, it was not from the car rental business. He saw the opportunity in the mobile phone industry, took it, and as they say, the rest is history.

I bought quite a few second hand buses from a dealer in Scotland, Blythewood's Motors, situated in one of Glasgow's well know streets Sauchiehall street. On one occasion the bus I was collecting was not ready, so I was advised that there's a café across the road, go and get yourself a bite and a drink. A tramp came and sat at the next table, and started to make conversation, "Where you're from Laddie," I answered politely, "Ah you're from England where about," again I answered politely, but not really wanting to make small talk, as I was sure he was going to ask for money for his next drink, "I said Stoke on Trent," his reply surprised me; "Potteries, I know it well, Burslem, Hanley, Stone, Longton, but when I'm in that area, I always use this great hotel in Lovatt Street."

I realised he stayed in the Salvation Army Hostel, but I did feel ashamed of myself, the poor bloke only wanted to talk, there was no tap up, he sat there quite happy eating his bowl of soup, I did offer to buy him a mug of tea, which he declined.

I also had two appearances at the Tribunal for unfair dismissal; the first one in my opinion was a farce. Each driver was allocated their own bus, they had to keep it clean and report any defects. We had a week's tour to Cliftonville, John Lewis was the driver, his allocated vehicle was a Ford Duple forty five seater. The tour was programmed to depart from the Shelton Gas Works club, on a Saturday morning. John had met the tour organiser beforehand, and had arranged to take his wife with him. I had no problem with that. Saturday came, he departed the depot, no problems. Two hours later, I had the dreaded telephone call, the bus has broken down, mad scramble round and send another bus out, and arrange to have the broken down one recovered and bought back to base.

The engine had seized up, on examination we found that the cause of the engine failure, was an engine core leaking, a fault that could have been rectified in a very short time and at a low cost. It appeared that the driver was fully aware of the problem, and had been continuingly topping up with water on his previous day's work, but thought that because his bus was faulty I would have allocated the job to another driver, with another bus. When the tour returned I made contact with the organiser, she explained that as soon as they got onto the Motorway, the bus started filling up with fumes (I should explain that the engine was front mounted, and could be accessed from the cab). He put a blanket over the engine cover, it's a wonder the bus didn't catch fire.

So here we are one week later, and to summarise, I had had to buy a replacement engine, at a cost of about two thousand pound's, the cost of the recovery, plus I lost the use of a bus for about a week, all this could have been avoided in a simple conversation, so you can understand why I was not the happiest person around. On interviewing him, I gave him a week's notice, he then signed on the dole, and I was taken to the Industrial Tribunal for unfair dismissal, and he won. The tribunal's view was that his actions did amount to gross misconduct, but gross misconduct was instant dismissal. I had failed to carry out the correct procedure by giving him notice, as we walked out of the court, my comments to him, was that he may have won, but they didn't say when I had to pay him, he had to take me to the County Court, which I made sure was a very long winded affair.

The other case was later when I was manager at Crystal Coaches, so I'll tell you about that when I get to it.

I applied to Staffordshire Moorlands District Council to use a short wheel base Ford Transit Minibus as a Taxi, and was refused, on the grounds that it didn't meet the requirements of the "Constructions of Use" regulations. This was 1974 fast forward to 2013 and half the Taxis on the road are based on short wheel base minibuses, where did I go wrong? Was I ahead of my time?

I was also on the Motorway Police's list of operators that could cover breakdowns on the M6, a couple come to mind, there was the prestigious one, the Indian Cricket Team's coach broke down, and we took them to their hotel in London. Then there was the one that had been involved in an accident, the coach actually ran over a car! It was a Scottish express coach and the passengers had flight connections at Heathrow. I remember this one because, as soon as my coach returned I had sent the invoice to the coach company, about three weeks later, I had a letter from BRS rescue saying reissue the invoice as is was payable by them, I did as they instructed, and got paid twice, nice earner.

But the one that made me laugh was a National Express coach going to Colne in Lancashire, it's windscreen had smashed, the Police control rang, and gave me all the details, where exactly it was, number of passengers, vehicle registration number, but she hadn't got the drivers name, then she had an inspiration, "He was the one with sticking plasters on his face!"

And so it came to pass that I was declared Bankrupt, this happened just before Christmas, 1986. The Inland Revenue petitioned me, which was fair enough, I'd had plenty of chances and warnings from them. At the hearing, because I was in employment, I had to make arrangements to repay my debtors, I was given instructions to contact the Official Receiver, a Mr Heavyside, after the holiday, to make suitable arrangements to repay. I left it until the end of January, well I didn't dare to leave it any longer, I then made contact with his office, and an appointment was made for me to attend their offices at 2 o'clock on a Wednesday. On the appointed day, we had a blizzard, so I rang their office to see if he had managed to get into work, no problem for me I only lived in Penkhull. Their offices were in Stoke, and was advised that due to the weather he was not in work, could I please ring in later to make another appointment, I mean would you? I know I certainly didn't, and I never heard another thing.

After three years I was entitled to automatic discharge, this was bought to my attention by the bankers of my employer, so acting innocent, but with the old heart pumping away, I made enquires, I thought Stanton, you could have to pay three years interest on top of any amount due! My enquires revealed that I had to go the County Court Buildings in Hanley, with my case reference, as you can imagine with the old knees knocking, I made my way to the reception desk, "Yes sir, no problem, however there's a fee to pay," wait for it, Thirty Pound's, I paid pronto and walked out completely free of debt and once again a valued member of society.

We have fast forwarded three years, lets go back to the actual day I was declared bankrupt, I can clearly remember saying to Linda, "That's fourteen years of my life wasted," however, I found out the following day, that other employers were willing to pay for my experiences, so I took up a position as Traffic Manager at Beresford's Buses, I can also remember picking up my first wage packet, and saying to Linda, "this is our money, we haven't got drivers asking for cash for a tyre or a battery etc., Linda I'm telling you now, that's it, I'm never going to be self employed again". Much to Linda's delight, and relief.

Job 33 Traffic Manager Beresford Motors

This was at the time of the Miners Strike, we were providing transport for Hem Heath, Wolstanton and Florence collieries, it was quite a nasty experience, and I don't think I would like to break picket lines again, but the job had to be done. A couple of incidents come to mind, the first, at Hem Heath. As I approached Hem Heath entrance it was obvious that there was both a large picket and Police presence, the pickets were very volatile, and the vehicles in front were being rocked and the occupants hassled. I sat back creating a gap then at full throttle made a sharp right turn and went into the pit through the exit gates. One of the picket leaders accompanied by a Police Officer came up to me, complaints were made that my driving was both dangerous and caused intimidation to the striking miners, the Police Inspector is telling me that I will be hearing from them, but at the same time he was winking at me.

On the return journey all the passengers were lying on the floor, this was the practice so that they wouldn't be recognized, I drove out through the gates with no problems, however as I turned left onto the main road, bang the windows were put in, I didn't stop. I can't recall any problems at Florence; however, Wolstanton was subject to visits by Flying Pickets, mainly from the North East, and believe me it's a terrifying experience to have to drive slowly through crowds, all the time being spat at and verbal threats made to you. The Flying Pickets were given the use of their fellow trade unions comrades facilities at the PMT Hanley Bus Station canteen, I've always believed in leading by example and to prove a point to my drivers, that we were just a face to them in a hostile environment, after driving through these lines of chanting miners and their threats, I parked my bus up at Hanley Bus Station, walked into the canteen, ordered breakfast and sat amongst them, point proved.

A couple of days later, same job, same crowd, after we had driven in though the pickets, I was approached again by a Police Inspector, he asked me if I was in charge, this guy was livid, and after he explained his reason, he wasn't on his own, one of my drivers, from the safety of his cab, had brandished a twenty pound note and a wage packet. As the police rightly said, this action made a difficult job, into a dangerous job. On the return to depot I gave the driver two options, option one,

Finish, Option two, donate the Twenty pound note to the striking miners fund, he chose to donate anonymously.

Let's leave the miners, and talk about how stupid one man could be, I had a new driver start, and he had only just passed his PSV test, paid for by him, but had no previous experience of working on the buses. He appeared keen, he even came in his own time to do route training, no adverse reports came back, come Saturday he's there ready to do a shift on Longton – Leek, pay as you enter. I went through his schedule with him, explaining about the canteen facilities etc., "Yes" was the answer, he understood everything required of him, so off he went. I was doing another route that came past the garage at about 3 pm. Immediately my attention was drawn to a bus parked up, so I got out to investigate, it was the new driver's bus, which was scheduled to finish about 6ish. Nothing I could do, until I saw the driver, he came in Monday morning bright as a button; acting if everything was ok, he wasn't aware that he'd done anything wrong. What he had done, was just drive up and down the shift's schedule, no timing points, no departure times, no meal breaks, if there was ten trips to be operated over the ten hours, he'd done them in seven hours, but surprisingly his takings for the turn were quite good.

One cold foggy January afternoon I was operating the Longton–Coalville service, I had arrived at Coalville, turned around and parked on the bus stop.

Luckily the coach was empty, there was snow on the ground and visibility was reduced, when without any prior warning I was flung out of my driving seat. I picked myself up off the floor, and looked down the bus. There was a lorry embedded, into the rear of my coach. I ran round to see if I could do anything, the other driver had blood coming out his eyes, I went into shock, and a crowd began to gather. Someone had called the emergency services, so I sat on the coach. I felt such a fool, if I tried to speak, tears welled up in my eyes, a nearby resident came to me, she knew me from Stallington Hospital days,   (not a patient) and said "Bill you look terrible, come with me and have a brandy."

All I could say, without crying, was. "No leave me alone." The Police arrived and breathalysed me, good job I didn't have that drink. The lorry driver claimed he skidded in the snow and ice, however as the police pointed out, there were no skid marks. They thought that he had fallen asleep, and as far as I know, no charges were bought against him, he was punished enough, after all he had lost an eye! Jimmy Beresford came out, and could see that I was in shock. At the scene of the accident he asked me to go and fill his car up, at the time this seemed unreasonable, however I realized that his motives were for me to drive straight after the accident was so I would not to lose my driving confidence.

At Beresford's we used to do troop movements, mainly from the Swynerton Barracks, or the Anzio Camp at Blackshaw Moor. This particular job was from Blackshaw Moor returning troops to the West coast of Scotland, North as far as Glasgow then down to Campbeltown. Do I hear you say, Campbeltown never heard of it, but if I was to call it Mull of Kintyre, you may have heard of it through the Paul McCartney's song, The Mull of Kintyre? The route from Glasgow was absolutely breathtaking; it was as though the sea was banging against your wheels. You think ah Glasgow at 6 pm, I'll soon be there but it was 9.45 pm, when I arrived. It was a two driver job, myself and Dennis Banner an old friend and ex-employee. So a quick wash and change of clothes, and we're off to the local Orange Club, where we were made welcome, well after all we'd bought their lads back.

The entertainment that night was the Bagpipes, now whether is was the alcohol or not, I don't know, but I really enjoyed it, in fact at the interval I made myself known to the piper, who told me that he was the Drum Major on the record 'Mull of Kintyre'. I told him that I'd enjoyed it that much I'd let him buy me a whisky, which he promptly did, in fact he bought me two, he had glanced at my table, which sported both a half empty glass, and another a full one, but only one of them was mine! But it would have been rude to refuse such hospitality, so Dennis and I staggered out of the club at about 1.30 in the morning, the 8 am start didn't materialise, more like 10 a.m.

I promised Linda I would take her on this journey one day, which I did, on my alleged retirement (a terminology coined by my children). I bought a motor home and planned a month's holiday touring Scotland, however as my 65th approached, Linda's health problems ruled this out, but we did manage to go to Campbeltown, it was everything as I'd described, plus the weather was perfect. We parked up at this site, and you could only hear two sounds, one was the gentle lapping of the sea, and the other was the bee's buzzing! Sadly we only had a week, and the Orange Club, is now housing.

I'd like to think that I did a good job at Beresford's, but after a few months I was approached by Julian Peddle who offered me a job at a company he had just purchased, Crystal Coaches. Now when someone approaches you, you can get a good deal, well I know I certainly did. I told Jim Beresford I was leaving him and joining Crystal Coaches as their Manager. Jim asked about the job offer, I told him the pay, "I'll match it" he replied, "pay me overtime", same response, "three weeks paid holiday", again Jim said "Yes", then I said company car, Jim's response, "I'll make you one." You would have had to known Jim to appreciate that comment!

He even said "Bill you know I've only got one child, a daughter, who's not interested in buses (she is a Doctor), I was rather hoping that you could see your future here," I thought thanks, but no thanks. Sadly Jim died shortly after. He was one of life's eccentrics, but also a gentleman. Immediately on his death, the business was sold to the PMT.

Job 34 Depot Manager, Stevenson's of Uttoxeter Ltd. T/A Crystal Coaches

Where do we start? Let's start off with the boss, Julian Peddle. A man I greatly admire, he had the knack of leaving it to you, in other words, delegate. He left you to it, but you knew he was there in the background watching and listening, this is a quality few men possess. He approached me to run his newest addition to the Stevenson's empire, and run it I did. Its main attraction (in my opinion) was that it was the contractor for Trusthouse Forte, at Keele Motorway Service Station. Crystal had been purchased from Tony Myatt, who I was already familiar with, although the premises at Newcastle were close to my home, (I lived at Penkhull,) it was a nightmare to operate from, especially as we expanded.

The staff I inherited were a very good bunch of lads, all characters in their own ways, Alan (Fit) the mechanic, drivers, Percy & Gordon all had to adjust to new owners and new management, but adjust they did, fitting in well within the Stevenson Group. As we began to expand taking on new drivers and additional vehicles it was obvious that we needed more space, it was particularly bad when the vehicles returned late, this was because we were situated opposite a night club. We even used to have cars parked in our yard, quite often we would have no option but to block them in, then we would have the problem of getting our vehicles out the following morning. It was often the case that people would sleep in them, and other activities. We have seen people wander down the entry and use it as a toilet, male and female, day and night.

Then there was the period of having a coach stolen, and then abandoned, usually in the Bignall End area, we never caught them. On more than one occasion we had Police sitting in the buses but nothing. Then one night, they were spotted driving off in a Leyland Leopard Coach, not the fastest of vehicles, a Police panda car took up the chase, and believe it or not, lost it, it was found as per normal in Bignall End, but it didn't happen again.

When the vehicles came in at night, they had to reverse into the parking area, and then before locking the bus up, drivers had to sweep it out leaving it clean for the next day, the reversing procedure was not the easiest due to both other vehicles coming up the street but the lack of space was at a premium.

One night at just turned half eleven at night I was in bed asleep, when the Police rang, asking details about the driver who had been on the Kidsgrove Adult Training Centre contract, as one of the attendees was missing. The police described her as a very vulnerable young woman; she was a resident of a home in Brindley Ford.

In response to their questions, I said, "No it was not possible that she was either with the driver, or she was still on the bus, after all the bus had been parked up since half past four, some seven hours earlier, plus the driver would have been aware of any passengers when he manoeuvred his bus into the limited space, plus again, he would have swept the bus out." The Police thanked me for this information, explaining that they had to try me before involving the forces helicopter. I lay in bed and thought for my piece of mind I'll go and check it out, yes, you've all guessed it, she was sitting on the bus, it was pitch black, I asked her if she was alright, she answered, "Yes I've been doing the ironing." As you can imagine the driver was subjected to a lot of ridiculing, comments like, "Did she pick her feet up for you when you swept out," and "Did she watch you back,"

I even submitted the story to the Stevenson's in-house magazine along with another snippet of useless information; this was about a coach party I had taken to the Queen's Hotel Blackpool. I had overheard one of my elderly passengers at the reception desk asking, "What floor is the first floor on?"

Talking about drivers, if I had a private hire, if possible I would try and tie it in with the Keele Services contract, 10-15 pm from Newcastle, wait and return at 11.10pm. This particular night the driver had to pick up a party from the Abbey Hulton area and take them to a pub at Chase Terrace, which was not far from Cannock, drop them off, do the Keele Job, and then pick them up afterwards. They had booked it for half past eleven return, but the woman organiser was a friend of mine, and she wasn't to bothered about the return time, give or take an hour.

Again, I'm in bed it's nearly one in the morning, and the Police are knocking at my front door. It was an old school chum, Frank, he said, "Bill, it was on our radio, that a coach party had not been picked up, when they said the name of the firm I thought I'd come and inform you," I answered him something like, "Thanks but it isn't a problem, it's probably old information." Thirty minutes later Frank's back, "Bill, I have them on the radio now, they are still there," It's now 01.30 in the morning, so off I go down to the depot and jump in a coach, the mystery deepens, the other coach is still out!

When I arrived in Cannock, I found a Policeman in a panda car, I woke him up. He looked at me, and at my coach, and says, "What the bloody hells going on, I've been riding round Cannock with another one of your buses, trying to find a pub party," I explained what was going on, now remember the driver had taken them, I didn't know where, but I did have the name of the pub, the Police Officer said, " Ever likely we couldn't find it, it's not in Cannock, its Chase Terrace about ten miles away." I dropped the last passengers off at 6 am, they were alright especially as I had refunded the coach money, and of course they had had plenty of booze. When I got back to the Depot there was a note on my car windscreen, it said, "Bill sorry about that, I suppose I've got the sack," I thought too true you have.

Later when he tried to explain it, his excuse was, that he had followed their directions to the pub, and as soon as he pulled up, they all dashed off the bus, and he forgot to ask the name of the pub or the area. I confirmed that as he had predicted, he was indeed sacked. The following day, for a sympathy vote he bought his wife and their new-born child, (when I say new-born, his wife had just given birth, and he was returning her home from the maternity hospital) to the office begging for his job, I'd have thought more of him if he had at least had the decency to take his wife home first.

I'd never heard of a coach driver forgetting where his party was, and I could not have had any confidence in his abilities again, so he became an ex-employee. Another employee George Bird, a character, but his heart was in the right place, he came to me asking for a job, at that time we didn't have any vacancies, I said that I'd bear him in mind. George offered to do any kind of work that became available, I asked if he was interested in a spot of labouring, "No problem," was the reply.

The job I offered him was laying a concrete base, at my home. I had bought a second hand, sectional concrete garage, this was nothing to George he was an expert, (he claimed). He promptly came and measured the job up, ready for an immediate start. He told me the amount of concrete that would be needed, I rang up and quoted cubic yardage as per George's instructions, and was quoted two hundred pound's, I said, "You must be joking, I haven't paid that much for the garage," they asked "What size is the garage?," when I told them they laughingly informing me that cubic yardage I had asked for would have been more suitable for a car showroom.

Shortly after this a vacancy did occur, and he duly joined our ranks, I had to send him home a couple of times to get changed. Once, he was proudly sporting a Tee Shirt with the message 'Bullocks to the pole tax,' (I've spelt it wrong, it wasn't spelt wrong on the shirt!) The other time he came with large overcoat type buttons sewn on the outside of his trouser fly hole! Then there was the time I had to go to his home for some reason, one of his sons was sitting on the front step, sucking a hose pipe, then spitting out water, he was empting the fish tank! Another time I had to give him an official warning, following a complaint from Keele Services. Our drivers bringing workers into Keele at the start or end of shifts, were allowed free meals, George's preference was KFC's, but as you can imagine at times queues formed. He would stand in the queue and shout his order, "Fillet Burger with no shit on it." Some thought it funny, others didn't, myself being one of the latter, but here we are some twenty nine years later and he's still bus driving, in fact I'm told that he's the Union Shop Steward.

Remember Terry Holmes the travel agent? Well, we were doing a job for him, picking up at Manchester Airport, at 11.00 at night. Same old Terry, only this time he'd got the days wrong. As per usual I was in bed when he rang me, "Bill, where's the bus at Manchester?" I replied "Terry that's tomorrow night," silence then, "But I meant tonight, can you tell them that you've been broken down, but Bill don't tell them the truth, I've explained you've had a breakdown". So off I set, and guess what, I did break down! What now? I'm the one who sorts out problems, and I'm stuck on the side of the M6, I had to ring up our MD Julian, who bought me a replacement bus out from Uttoxeter.

It was about 4.30 in the morning when we rolled up at the airport, and I was met by a very irate crowd, I said, "Let me put your cases in the boot and I will explain to you all before we depart." So, I stood at the front of the bus, and said, "As you all know I broke down on the M6, I made my way to the emergency telephones to report it, and I was asked by the operator what the problem was, I was told to go back to my vehicle and await help. After waiting a considerable time I went back to the telephone, and asked what was happening, this time I was put through to the Police, who sincerely apologised, explaining that the telephone number I had supplied to contact my employers had been copied down wrong, I had told them Uttoxeter 2131, and they had been trying Uxbridge 2131". I could feel the sympathy for me, and believe it or not I even had a collection, when we got back Julian said, "I'll never believe a word you say again, you were that convincing!"

Job 35 Car & truck parts salesman

In conversation with the former owner of Crystal Coaches, Tony Myatt, he told me he was leaving the area, as he had purchased a chip shop in Camber Sands. Now, I knew that he also had another business Tip Top Autos that supplied ANC the parcel firm with their replacement parts. I asked what was happening to Tip Top, he said "Nothing, you can have it if you want it." Two problems to this first, Stevenson's, I approached Julian who agreed as long as my work at Crystal wasn't affected, then he had no objection, the second one was ANC. This company was founded by an ex-policeman, as was Tony Myatt, now we were known to each other having clashed in our former business interests, me B Cabs, him City Radio Cabs.

Tony arranged a meeting to see if an agreement could be made between the two of us, to my surprise he agreed to me coming in, his comments were; that as I already knew, Mrs Robinson, (remember Robinsons Taxis) had come to him seeking advice about my threats of making her bankrupt, his advice had been to her, to ignore me, that in his words, "I hadn't got the balls", but he was wrong, I did make her bankrupt, and because of that, as far as business was concerned he respected me!, Strange world isn't it? Tip Top Autos did very well, but then ANC discovered that because all the vehicles were in fact on lease agreements, that they were not responsible for replacement parts, so I changed the name to Tip Top Chemicals, and supplied them with cleaning materials. I also put in a second hand hot water power wash machine, and they had free use of it as long as they purchased the soap from me. Then that increased to two machines, both second hand, one got stolen and they replaced it with a new one.

It was a good business, I had no overheads, and the profit margins were good, until I took on a partner, Derek Dawson, (the mobile mechanic who I have previously mentioned). He was now however a chemical salesman working for a firm in Cardiff. I bought some TFR from him, he claimed to turn over fifteen thousand pounds per month, and if I were to join forces with him, he could quite easily double this figure. I thought to myself, he's a salesman, allow for exaggeration, if his monthly turnover is nearer the eight thousand mark, I will still be able to increase my profits, so I went ahead, forming a limited company, called Mapleshore Ltd, trading as Tip Top Chemicals, 60% shares for me and 40% for him.

I supplied him with a company car etc., but he never hit any where near his suggested turnover. The best month he had, was about two and a half thousand pound's, I was doing that without leaving the office. He was very smartly dressed and could talk the talk, he claimed to be an ex-SAS man, and was still on call if required, he would claim that he had been down to Hereford to meet up with lads, and even showed up one day, in an Army Captain's uniform, complete with a pistol, ammunition and a Bren gun! He would drive into the yard like a boy racer, wheels spinning, and then do a handbrake turn. It was impossible to contact him the afternoons, eventually I found out why; he was a very accomplished golfer. If I remember right his handicap was four. I also found out all this hard man lark was a front.

When I lost my temper with him one day, (it was to do with the loading of a van), anyway I lost it, and to my surprise he was all mouth. Shortly after this I sacked him; he claimed that I couldn't as he was a forty percent shareholder in the business; to get round this I gave him, very reluctantly, the car in exchange for the shares. A couple of months later our Keith picked us up from Manchester Airport, we had been to America on holiday, and on the way back he told me what had happened to Derek. Whilst we had been away, he'd been masquerading as an Army Officer at the Blackshaw Moor Army Training camp, in a uniform he had bought from the Army Surplus Store. I never found out about the guns, but he had never been in the Forces or as he a claimed a Police Officer, and when he worked for the police it was a mechanic, not as he had claimed, a Police Officer.

His wife I had known for years, before she had even met him; she told me that they were getting a divorce as he used to knock her about, however he died of a heart attack, he was only in his early fifties.

Mapleshore Ltd carried on, I gave Linda his shares, I was still employed by Stevenson's, but by this time we had moved to purpose built premises, at Hot Lane Industrial Estate. Again Julian had given me permission to carry on using the premises for my other business interest Tip Top Chemicals, things were hectic, as you can imagine, Stevenson's were busy and so was Tip Top, so it didn't help matters when one Sunday night, Linda and I had been for a drink at the Royal Oak in Dilhorne.

I had had my customary three halves, driving home as we approached Cellarhead cross roads, the lights were on green, as I was driving through I was suddenly aware of a car to my right coming through on red, a collision was unavoidable, thankfully we were not hurt. I called the police as it was obvious that other driver was under the influence, but I will admit to be terrified myself, even though I had called the Police and had only three halves, you are asking yourself is three halves safe? When the Police arrived, well that in itself, was in a way comical, it was if they were on elastic, for three squad cars arrived at the same time, one from the direction of Leek, one from Cheadle, and the other from Longton. After questioning me, the Police said to me "Right you can go," I thought to myself, wow they haven't breathalysed me!, right I'm off, but first I commented on the damage to my car, and would I be alright to drive it in that state, the Police said "Yes, if you are stopped just tell them you were the other vehicle that was in the RTA at Cellarhead."

I thought great, let's go, but then I had to work out a route from Cellarhead to Penkhull that didn't involve any sharp left hand turns, as the front wing was touching the tyre. Let's change the topic and relate a couple of amusing incidents. Every Wednesday night myself and a few of the lads would meet up at the Victoria Pub, May Bank, for a few drinks and a chat, usually about work, but we were always up for a laugh. The first one involved Tony Bagguley, (Bag Pus) he worked for us on a part time/casual basis, his full time occupation was as a Fireman, on this occasion he bought along a colleague from the Fire Service of Bermuda, who had been on a training course with them at Newcastle, and was due to go back. Tony was for ever the practical joker, he decided that he would play a joke on this guy, as drinks were bought he was told that it was an old English custom, to raise your glass, and shout out a toast. So as you can imagine the pub was in uproar, as every time he filled his glass up, we all shouted out the toast, which was Bollocks!. But this stunt backfired on Tony, as the following night, the guy from Bermuda was invited to the Fire

Chiefs house, to meet his family and enjoy dinner, so as the glasses were clinked instead of the customary "Cheers", their was a load shout of "Bollocks", the Fire Chief immediately asked, "been out with Bag Pus?"

We had a part time driver named Bill Wade, I'll be kind and say he was fond of the ale, when ever he came to us he would always follow the same pattern, come on the bus and a taxi home, so when Bill said his goodnights at about eleven, nothing else was thought about it, until the Landlord approached us, apparently about half an hour later he had gone to lock up, did a visible check outside, and spotted a body lying on the grass.

Yes it was Bill, he had gone out to catch his Taxi, walked over the lawn, and miscalculated the height of the chain, in his drunken state he couldn't get up, and after a brief struggle gave up and went to sleep, our Keith went out and came back with the giggles, as he bent down to pick Bill up, there was a slug crawling over his glasses! Back with Tony, he had a side kick who we called Magnolia, he came by this name because helping Tony on a decorating job, Tony sent him for a tin of Magnolia Emulsion, and he came back with white, he claimed he couldn't say Magnolia, anyway one Wednesday night he was the victim of Tony's sense of humour. Tony claimed that he could hypnotise him, he used an empty beer bottle and placed a lit candle underneath it, Magnolia was instructed to wait until the bottle cooled down, then place the base to his eye, first the left then the right. Magnolia was in his element as in his opinion Tony had failed to hypnotise him, I gave the show away by asking, "Tony what does your Panda want to drink".

By now you will have worked out that Magnolia was not the brightest spark about, take for instant when his wife left him, he went and had a vasectomy reversal in case he met a nice girl, then there was the time he came into the bus yard one day on his motor bike, bang straight into the garage doors, we picked him up, and asked if was ok, he replied "yes, but is Alan (The fitter) in", his brakes didn't work!

Closing time at the Vic was eleven o'clock, but we were alright for at least another hour, on this particular night Alan and myself had left the pub at about eleven forty five, the following morning we were both surprised to learn that a fight had started after we had left and one man had been murdered, it was Michael Smith, who at one time had worked for me, I had spoken to him in the pub, but being as I'd sacked him, it wasn't what you could call a spirited conversation. I did have to make a statement relating to the incident, but it was cut and dried relating to the people who were involved, but it put a stop to the late night drinking.

It was shortly after this that a couple of things were happening with Stevenson's, I had been negotiating an annual increase in rates at the Keele Motorway Service Area, and this had been refused. I had suggested a reduction in vehicles for the same rate, Keele were happy to consider this, Julian was not. I had been in talks with Jim Stonier, his business was in dire straights, and would I consider becoming involved in it? The business actually consisted of Jim, his three sons, and a rented yard in Shelton. Under normal circumstances it was a no goer, but he been offered the Coalville to Hem Heath miners contract, and basically he couldn't afford to do it, so I did a deal with him. I would buy the business of J.W. Stonier & Sons, based on the turnover, which was thirty thousand pounds, but with no money upfront. I would guarantee him and his sons a wage, plus I would gradually repay him the thirty grand, out of future takings, which was accepted. The alternative would have been that Stoniers would have ceased trading; Jim in his seventies still had a mortgage!

Julian was kept in the picture of my intentions and was quite happy for me to negotiate with Keele Services, so I parted company with Stevenson's. Oops I nearly forgot to tell you about the second appearance at the Industrial Tribunal for unfair dismissal, this was an old buddy of mine from the PMT days, known to one and all as Knocker.

On this particular day he had been on a school journey, collecting the older children from Madeley High School, and then the younger ones from Baldwins Gate, returning them to Norton Bridge. The children themselves could be quite boisterous, anyhow, on this occasion my phone was red hot with complaints about the driver, so I was of course waiting for him. His explanation of the incident didn't ring true, a number of the children had cut lips etc., he claimed that a car had braked in front of him, causing him to brake sharp, because of the number of complaints I decided to suspend him, pending further investigations. The following morning accompanied by Julian, I did the route and met the angry parents; it appeared that my theory of the incident suited the facts more than his account. Now Knocker was a friend of many years, I said to him "Just tell us the truth," I also said to him, "I have on many occasions had to tell the children to sit down, and even threatened to report them to the school," this I might add, made no difference.

My interpretation of the incident was that he touched the brakes to make them sit in their seats, but he denied this and stuck to his version of the event. This left me with no other option but to dismiss him, and I was duly done for unfair dismissal. The tribunal was held in Birmingham, Julian accompanied me, but on this occasion the tribunal found in my favour, their verdict was that after listening to all the evidence from both parties, Mr Stanton's version of the event seemed to be the most appropriate and again Mr Stanton seemed to be the most truthful witness. As we walked out of the court Knocker came up to me, shook hands with me, saying, "Sorry about this Bill, but my dole would have been stopped if I hadn't gone ahead with it," anyway, I did have a drink with him again, and there were no hard feelings.

Job 36 Coach Operator J.W Stonier & Sons, Old Mill Garage, Shelton New Road

Tip Top Chemicals moved to the yard at Shelton, the contract for Hem Heath was safely under the belt, as was Keele Services, now for Jim and his lads, and their ramshackle buses. It must have been a shock to the system for them to have regular work, in fact the eldest son refused to even start working for me, the youngest son, was the fitter, and he was semi-skilled. Now because of my background history with the Ministry and the history of Stoniers I had to be very careful with our maintenance system, and it would be fair to say that several stand up arguments took place, but there could only be one winner, me, so eventually the youngest and I parted company. That left father and one son, Graham. Graham was a first class worker, and was with me till the sell out.

Now, Jim, this was hardest thing I have ever had to do, it started at Hem Heath Pit. Jim was on the Coalville route, and I was doing another run, we arrived at the pit bringing in the noon shift, arriving there at about 1pm, and then we had to wait to take the day shift home, about two hours later. There would have been about five or six other drivers there, we all sat in the canteen, but not Jim, he spent the entire two hours plus, pacing up and down the bus. I formed the opinion that he was mentally sick. Now this was the hard bit, how do you tell a person this, but it had to be done, so that night after a long discussion I finished him, I promised him, that although he would not have a wage as such, I would pay him a weekly amount from the previous agreement, within three days he was admitted to Cheddleton Mental Hospital as he had had a nervous breakdown!

I hadn't been there long when I received a tip off that someone was stealing diesel from the premises at night, so for about a month I sat in Cemetery road from midnight until about 4am. I chose Cemetery Road because it gave me an ideal viewing position. Eventually my patience was rewarded, a large van reversed down to the depot, I immediately rang 999, and blocked the van in, I caught him climbing over the wall into my premises, with a couple of five gallon containers. The Police arrived, he claimed he had only stopped to relieve himself, the cans were not his and he denied climbing over the fence. The

Police advised me that nothing could be proved and gave him a warning, but no more fuel went missing. It was suggested at the time that an employee of mine was involved. But again nothing could be proved, however, I had recognised the van, but not him, he kept the van in an area that was familiar to me, shall we just say that the van must have had an expensive engine repair!

Included in the takeover I not only inherited the buses, but also a dog, called Juno, and an old dilapidated static caravan, that had at one time been home to Jim. Let's talk about Juno first, he was a huge, soft Rottweiler, he was impossible to secure, his neck was wider than his head! I had to put a rope under his front legs tied to his collar. One day we tied him to a scrap Ford Transit Diesel engine and gearbox, he just walked about pulling it behind him! I was out walking him one day, past the old Twyford's factory, when I met an old friend, Alan Jones (ex-Lord Mayor). We stopped to chat but I could see that Alan was intimidated by Juno, but on my command "Juno sit," no problem the dog just sat there good as gold, however, I could see that Alan was still a little agitated, Juno was sitting on his foot!

The dog was supposed to be a guard dog, if it was cold he wouldn't leave his kennel, in fact the night of the diesel incident, he never left his kennel, even when the police arrived, any intruder would have been licked to death. Sadly one morning when I arrived at the depot he had got out of the yard and was found dead in the road, the victim of car/van accident, whatever had hit him, it would have received extensive damage.

Let's get back to the office, it was in such a poor state of repair that it had to be scrapped, we stripped it down and sold the metal, the interior I decided to burn, along with some old coach seats, and boy did it burn. The bus yard was situated behind a Petrol Station, when the fire brigade arrived they claimed that they could see the smoke from the Fire Station in Hanley, two miles away! I was lectured on the dangers of fire and warned to my future conduct, it was pointed out to me that even though I had lit the fire in an open yard, (facing the canal) it could have been fatal, as the coach seats were constructed with a very high foam content, and the fumes from these were not only poisonous but tended to lie low, their parting words were that I was lucky to be alive.

This brings me to the replacement office; I purchased another static caravan from a farm between Chesterton and Audley. Frankie Johnson a friend of mine, offered to tow it back with his Transit Van, so early one Sunday morning we set off. Frank towing the caravan, me behind with my hazard lights on, straight down the A500, no problem, and into Shelton New Road, now to reverse into the depot, as soon as he attempted this, the caravan's A frame crumpled up, it was as rotten as a pear, so we had to man handle it into position, discussing it afterwards with Frank I asked him, "What would he have done if it had come adrift on the journey?" he replied, "Get the hell out the area."

The phone call came one lunch time, one of my buses had reversed over a woman at Keele Services. I dashed to Keele and saw that the ambulance was still in attendance. What had happened was that the bus bringing the workers in as per contract had been involved in a collision with a female passenger off a tourist coach, she had joined this coach in Preston and was travelling to Germany. I do believe this was at the time a regular weekly bus service, Scotland to Germany calling at various pickups. The coach had arrived at Keele and the crew were taking a break, the lady had alighted from the coach reading a book, not realising that due to the fact the vehicle she was travelling in was left hand drive, and she had in fact stepped off into the traffic, not the kerbside. This happened as my bus was reversing in; she had several bruises and grazes but refused hospital treatment, and after receiving treatment from the paramedics carried on with her journey to Germany.

Two weeks later she returned from her holiday, and promptly claimed off my insurance company. The first I knew about any claim, was in correspondence from my insurance company, she was held 60% at fault, well I hit the roof, to get off a coach reading a book on a busy Motorway Service Area, is in my opinion tantamount to attempted suicide, so why we were held responsible in any way? This was because my bus was not fitted with reversing aids, horn, beeper etc., they paid her eighteen thousand pound's because in their words, it was cheaper than defending it in court!

Both Stoniers and Tip Top were doing well, I was now banking with the Yorkshire Bank, who had approached us, and I remember Linda being impressed that the Bank Manager actually visited us to get our business. Until then I was banking with the Royal Bank of Scotland, but Linda's Mum and Dad, had asked us if we were interested in buying their house, under the government's scheme of 'Council house tenants right to buy'. I approached the RBOS to see if they would lend me the six and a half thousand pound's we needed, however, I still owed Barclays Bank fourteen thousand from my bankruptcy, they agreed to loan me the money, but I would have to borrow the amount of twenty thousand five hundred, to pay off Barclays first. Along came the Yorkshire who were happy to loan me the six and a half thousand pounds, this I think you'll agree with me, was a no brainer.

So 271 Beaconsfield Drive was purchased. I paid off the loan in a year, I then approached Barclays concerning the debt of over fourteen thousand pound's, pointing out that although I was paying them a set monthly amount to reduce the debt and had in fact voluntary increased the agreed monthly payments, the deal that I had with them, was 'No interest,' and would take me a further twelve years to finalise the debt. The total outstanding amount at the time was in the region of twelve thousand pound's, I offered them five thousand pounds as a full and final payment (again to be borrowed from the Yorkshire) they agreed to accept five and a half thousand pounds. Linda always said this was one of the most pleasant things she has ever had to do; the look on the Bank Managers face was priceless when she walked into their offices at Festival Park and presented him with the Draft.

In fact our relationship with the Yorkshire was at such a level that the Manager would ring me up asking me for my opinion on other applicants, and we were even invited to a social evening, all expenses paid, at Hagley Hall in the West Midlands. It was an evening of Poetry starring Marion Montgomery, (a famous American Jazz singer of the time). I recall after the event I was asked if I had enjoyed the evening, I replied along the lines that is was not my cup of tea, and thank goodness I'm not an intellect, although to be fair, Linda did enjoy the evening.

Business was good as I had introduced Coaching, Contracts and Stage carriage work into our schedules; however we were effectually involved with a bus war with the PMT. I decided at a very early stage that we could not compete with them on the ground, if any of my buses were seen off their designated route both the driver and myself would be in trouble, and in fact would play into their hands, so I used the powers of publicity, letters to the Evening Sentinel both from myself and the public. As an example as a follow up to some comments in the Sentinel, I stated that the PMT in their "Bus War" against me, were using buses made in Germany, not like Stoniers using buses made in England, which in turn was supporting British industry, there were in fact Old Leyland Sherpa's, PMT were using Mercedes, never the less I scored the brownie points.

The PMT often diverted off the registered route, they would miss part of the route out, effectively taking shortcuts, this enabled them to get in front of our bus, illegal, but proving it was another matter, they had that many it would have been impossible to prove the fact. I often patrolled the route in my car, and if I spotted one of theirs off route I would follow it and make some observation of it, say a brake light out or a number plate dirty, I would then write to the depot manager at their depot, pointing out the defect, he would then reply thanking me. These letters were in my opinion confirming that the said vehicle had actually been where and when I had claimed, again on a couple of occasions, knowing that their vehicle had gone off route, and wearing a High Vis jacket I flagged their buses down, and informed the driver that I would be reporting them to the relevant authorities, although I never did.

On another occasion I stood at Porthill Church for four hours one morning taking photographs of the PMT buses and noting their timing, what they didn't know was that there was no film in the camera, but our takings were certainly up. The minibuses, as I've said were Leyland Sherpa's, my fleet colour was a deep red, however I purchased some replacement/additional ones from a dealer, they were ex Busy Bee's Manchester, who like the PMT were a subsidiary of National Bus, so operated in the same colour scheme.

PMT were furious with me, saying I was trying to pass off as them, and if I didn't immediately repaint them, they would issue a high court injunction against me. To the untrained eye I appeared to be ignoring them, I actually kept one in its original colours, repainting the others but operating them out of their sight, well, where possible, anyway it worked. The PMT went too great expense taking a high court action against me, but I of course took great pleasure in showing them the one outstanding vehicle going into the paint shop. But the one thing that upset them the most was when I commissioned a graphic designer to print some vinyl's of Chickens, which I plastered down the sides of the buses, together with the caption, Hop on a Cheepa bus from Stoniers. They were on the phone threatening me with all kinds of actions, saying I was insinuating that my fares were cheaper then theirs, (they had in fact instructed their drivers to match our fares, and issued them with the same ticket machines as ours) as per usual I took pleasure in reading them a letter from the days post, from a lady in Clayton who had wrote thanking Stoniers for charging children half fare, not like the PMT's two thirds (I think it was the Cheepa bus episode that made them decide to buy me out!).

On the funny side, we had a schedule that operated from Barlaston taking the children to School, the first day the bus appeared with the chickens down the side, all the children hopped on to the bus! As I've banded the phrase 'Bus wars' about, this was a common description around the country, not just with me. On one occasion I was being interviewed at Newcastle Bus Station by Central Television, the cameras were set up, and I asked the question, "Do I look at the Reporter or the Camera?" the answer was to ignore the camera and just act normal. Looking at the interviewer, as I began to discuss and answer the questions being put to me, I was aware that there was a spider on my glasses, I tried to ignore this fact, however the report was never shown, only the sound track was used, and that was on the local radio.

An opportunity came up to purchase a new depot, it was on the Parkhouse Industrial estate, Chesterton. It had been a project started by a building company, who had gone into receivership, it was only a shell with no services connected, however, with the Yorkshire Bank's backing I put in an offer, which eventually was accepted. Knowing of the area's reputation I had the building completed with no windows, this was to minimise the risk of burglary, wrong. They forced the fire door open, when I say forced, they actually ripped the door frame away from the wall!, sort that one out, no problem, we fitted a metal frame welded into position, so did that stop them, no, they got in through the roof.

At my old place I had my own Fork Lift Truck, which was a valuable asset especially with the forty-five gallon drums of cleaning chemicals, so I drove it from Shelton to Chesterton. As I was driving through Wolstanton along the High Street, I hit a pot hole and one of the forks fell off, it caused a bit of a traffic jam, but it didn't take long to sort out, but it was a maul. I had a massive safe fitted with an exterior drop chute so that the drivers could deposit their takings, without entering the building, plus every night before going home we would put the office typewriter and the diary in, they never managed to get into the safe.

Another operator in Stoke, Graham Shaw who operated as
Moorland Rover was in a similar battle with the PMT, he rang
me one day asking if I would approach the PMT with a buy out
proposition, as he had had enough!, I should add that at the
time I was the Chairman of the North Staffs Bus and Coach
Operators Society. The PMT were happy to discuss terms with
him, then out of the blue they asked me if I was interested in
selling out, my reply was "Make me an offer I can't refuse," so
they did, bear in mind I had only been operating Stoniers three
years. When I bought it, the yearly turnover was thirty
thousand pound's, when it was sold it was two hundred and
fifty thousand pound's. As I've said my approach was, make
me an offer, I didn't want to sell the depot just the business,
however, they insisted it had to be both the business and the
premises. This is where I slipped up, they asked me for a
valuation, I thought I was being clever and saving money,
when it was agreed that it would be o.k. for them to obtain a
fair valuation using their valuers, it was after all Louis Taylor's,
a very well respected company. With hindsight I should have
realised that they would act in their benefit, anyway, the price
for the business and vehicles was agreed upon, plus the depot
at valuation.

Come the day of the legal signing, I was to put it mildly,
disappointed, the figure for the garage did not take into

consideration all the work and connecting the services that had gone into it, so I said "No Deal", they were horrified, but managed to find another ten thousand pound's to secure the deal. What I didn't know was that the day they took me over, they themselves were also taken over by Badgerline. Although I do remember being surprised that the solicitors were still working at 7pm. So Stoniers became a part of the PMT, one of the deciding factors of selling up, was the drivers. Whilst I did on the whole have a good reliable driving force, others were not so good, and as the business expanded I had to employ some drivers that would not have usually met my criteria.

As I've said negotiations were long and at times complicated, however it had to be kept a secret, even from the workforce. When the deal was completed and on the final shift the workers were told, with the promise that each and every one was guaranteed a job, even though some had in the past been dismissed from the PMT. One driver Chris Brownsword, I was told, took exception to this, saying "I had sold them down the river," and what he was going to do to me was nobody's business. The fact that he would let us down on his late turn, on some flimsy excuse, like the wife has an headache, didn't count for anything, even though it was yours truly who had to do a double shift, working from 6 in the morning until 11.00 at night.

Shortly after the takeover, Linda and I were shopping in W H Smiths in Newcastle, when I spotted him, Linda said "Come on lets go, and of course I didn't, I went straight up to him, to be greeted with a friendly "How are you Mate," talk about two faced.

Job 37 Chemical Salesman.
I still had Tip Top Chemicals, and secured an operating base in Stone, Whitebridge Industrial estate, I took on the redundant staff from a failed Chemical Company. Mike Beech was the manager plus the sales force of Rita, Mark and Adrian and of course Big Andy, plus a telephone appointment maker (can't remember his name) and Roy Henny as my accountant, which left me with little to do. I was not used to having time on my hands, the sale to the PMT was subject to me having nothing to do with the bus industry within a thirty mile radius from base, for three years. So after three days I went to Keele Services where I had made many friends, to have a cup of coffee (free) and a chat.

Whilst I was there the Area General Manager, Brian Lotts, saw me, and greeted me with the comments, "What's up Stanton, are you bored?" I had to agree with his comments, for the truth of the matter was that I had no hobbies or other interests, as the buses were twenty four seven. Brian then said the words that was to change everything and alter my course of direction, his offer was that he would keep me occupied, I asked what was he offering, "Site Maintenance" "me?" I laughed, "I can't even put a screw in correctly!" Brian's answer was that "he wasn't bothered, he said that if I couldn't do a job, I had been in business long enough to know a man who could, so was I interested?"

Too true I was, it was agreed that I would be Mr Twenty per cent man, and it worked well. I started off as me being the errand boy, as a prime example I received a phone call that they had run out of mushrooms, off I went to the wholesalers in Newcastle, collected a box of Mushrooms which cost about two pound's fifty, my profit? Fifty pence! However the next call was for cans of pop and chocolate, Seven hundred pound's worth, get the picture? Also, general site work came up, like tiling and carpentry, and yes, I had the contacts to do this. Then I was offered the sites sewage contract, which had been operated by Newcastle Borough Council, I tendered and won the contract, this was a three hundred and sixty five day contract.

Every day someone had to check that the pumping station was functioning correctly, I of course knew nothing about this, but Newcastle council had made their man redundant, so I offered him a part time position, I would do the Monday – Friday and he would do the Saturday & Sunday, subject to him training me, which brings me too:-

Job 38 Sewage Operator

This worked well, as by and large we didn't have many problems, until one day, the system became blocked, this problem was not new, it had occurred several times before. Several valves had to be opened until the trapped air in the system was cleared, this time was different, the blockage must have been there for some considerable time, and the trapped air had become steam. As soon as I opened the valve hot steam shot out, onto my hand, causing me severe burns to my hand, an ambulance was called and Keele's first aider came to my rescue. She sat me down and placed my hand under running water, the skin promptly rolled off! I don't know who felt the worse me or her, anyway the ambulance arrived and I was promptly whisked off to hospital.

Linda was informed, she was at Cheadle, babysitting for my son, Keith, she immediately set off to the accident department, fearing the worse, as she approached the hospital, and there I was sitting on the wall, waiting for her. When I got into the car it soon came apparent why I had been treated so quickly, I was covered in shit, sorry but that's the only word that described it. I had to attend the burns unit a couple of times after, but it healed up with no side effects. We are now leading up to;

Job no 39 Electrician (sort of)

This contract entailed me every day at about 6 in the morning checking all the bulbs on site, and changing where necessary, plus the carpark lights, no problem with the interior lights but for the exterior ones I had to purchase a Cherry Picker. I asked the sites maintenance man, Frank, "How high do you think the lamp standards are?" Frank replied, "About twenty foot" so I went out and bought a Cherry Picker based on a Freight Rover Chassis. It had a height lift of sixteen foot.

So I reasoned, sixteen foot with a bloke in will be sufficient, come the big day and I'm proud of my acquisition. I positioned the vehicle in front of the offices to demonstrate, on hindsight I should have familiarised myself with the controls first, anyway, man in it, up it went, but it wouldn't reach. The operator shouted down, "It's about ten foot too short," and then bought it down.

Now what I hadn't realised was that the lift had a safety device fitted, and it had to be completely centralised before the stabilizing legs could be retrieved, so not knowing what I was doing, I stood on the back trying different handles, as I pressed one, the lift started going up, the handle stuck down, so I let go. When it reached its maximum height it stopped, but I couldn't get it down, luckily I had a couple of men subcontracting for me, that entailed ladder work; they went up their ladder and bought it down for me, all very embarrassing especially outside the offices. You will note that I didn't go in either the Cherry Picker or up the ladders, as I don't like heights. So the Freight Rover went back to the dealers, and I went to the auctions at Telford and purchased an ex-British Telecom Cherry picker this time with a forty five foot lift. I paid about two thousand five hundred pound's for it, took it to Keele and tried it out on the Lamp Standards. Up it went, again came the shout, "Bill its too short", I asked "How much?" Again the reply came, "About ten feet." Not so embarrassing this time, it was well away from the offices. So I put it back into the auctions and lost about a thousand pounds, so what next?

I bought a redundant fire engine, with a seventy five foot lift. It was an ERF with a Rolls Royce Petrol engine, with terrible brakes and a very thirsty engine. I paid six and a half thousand pound's for it, this time it was show off time, outside the offices again, up it went, no trouble, every one dead impressed, Brian Lotts amongst them. Right Bill try it on the other side, southbound, driving over the bridge to the other side, the damn thing ran out of petrol, it had used five gallons of petrol just going up to one lamp standard!

But it proved a willing workhorse, even though it was rarely used. I had it painted yellow, and it always attracted attention of people passing through, even the late Fred Dibnah came and showed interest in it, we offered a swop but he wasn't interested, (joke). Every day there was someone climbing over it, so I decided to park it up at a friends farm, Mario, who lived a couple of miles down the road, then another friend, Sid Broomfied, approached me asking if he could hire it, as he had encountered problems with Health and Safety on demolishing an area that was being developed into a building site, in Stone. (Fast forward to 2013 my eldest daughter Tracy has purchased one of these houses). The Fire engine satisfied their inspectors and the job was completed to their satisfaction, some time later Sid approached me asking to hire it again, as he had to demolish a chimney on a former Royal Doulton factory, in Tunstall, luckily I'd cleared it with the insurance company first, as one night it was torched, a resident of the nearby houses rang 999 and told them that a fire engine was on fire. The fire brigade decided as all their engines were accounted for, it must be a crank call, too late, the fibreglass cab was burnt to the ground and it was declared a total loss. Much to my amazement the insurance company on their first offer offered me six and a half thousand pound's, which is what I had bought it for, so I snatched their hand off, which brings me too;

Job 40 Toilet Cleaner

When I started at Keele it was owned by Trusthouse Forte, which was then taken over by Granada. I was asked to take over the sites cleaning schedules, which included the toilets, at one time I had twenty nine staff working there, both full and part time, this was as well as the other contracts, and Tip Top Chemicals. With the new owners came the sites refurbishment, which was carried out by a firm called Mancells. One day I was approached by their Site Manager asking if I could help them out by doing an Industrial Cleaning job in Burton on Trent, it was overnight and they were desperate, so yes we did it, which led me on to;

Job 41, Industrial Cleaner

This job led to many others mainly around the North West, we did numerous jobs around Liverpool, Preston, Blackburn, Bolton, Burnley, Manchester, Chester the last one being Wrexham. I used a different team of men on these jobs, mainly Mike Gent and his three sons, and because we were never at one place long the jobs were all very interesting, I think the longest one we were on was at the Albert Dock, Liverpool. This went on intermittently for about six months. It was a Gym conversion and was situated right above the Beatles Experience. Beatles music played every day from 9 in the morning till 6 at night, and the same songs over and over again, it was not my idea of heaven. As the job came to a conclusion it entailed some outside work, which required working on upper floor window ledges, so we had to wear safety harnesses. On this particular day, I was working on a ledge that recessed inwards, and I was working on steps, as I was climbing back into the building my heel caught the steps, which went flying through the air, and as they landed caught the windscreen of a parked van.

I made my way down, and apologised to the driver, who was a decent bloke, his reply was "No Problem Mate, it's chipped the Windscreen buts it's a hire van, and it's covered for that, I just won't tell how it happened". At that the docks the security man appeared with the Site manager, claiming that I'd thrown the steps down, this was the man who two days previously claimed that he hadn't seen a thing when my van had been broken into, all my tools and even the generator had been stolen, so I was pretty wound up. I was still wearing my safety harness, I said, "Actually the steps and I were going to commit suicide, the steps had jumped but I chickened out."

It was on this job when they told me where my next job would be, Toxteth, which as you may know is a notorious area. I expressed my concern pointing out that I had only just purchased replacement tools, they said, "Bill we understand your concerns, but we can guarantee you will have no problems, in fact you can leave your van with the keys in it." "How come?" I asked, and was told that the job would be at a Special School for Handicapped Children, and there is honour and respect in the area, and I never did have any trouble.

Having said that, one Sunday morning I did say to one of the contractors that there seemed to be a lot of Police in the area, "Ah yes" he said, "Someone got shot last night, just around the corner."

Another Liverpool job was at Cunard House, the caretaker gave me a guided tour, and it was fascinating, all the underground storage areas, not only for luggage but vast storage areas for coal, as the ships were coal fired. As he explained, "Say Lord Derby was going on a cruise, he would arrive with not only his entourage, but his valuables as well, as it would be common knowledge that he was out of the country." You can even see where the old docks were, I can't really do it justice here.

Liverpool is a fascinating city with some remarkable buildings, not only the exteriors but the interiors are also well worth viewing, and I had the privilege of working in a couple of these, namely Canada House, and the Council Offices in Dale Street. Canada House is situated opposite India House, the former passport office, and Mancells had the contract here to convert it for the Home Office to use as an Immigration centre. Whilst we were working there a film was being shot in Liverpool, starring Samuel H Jackson. I was told that on Sunday the road would be closed, but me being clever thought it wouldn't apply at 7am, wrong. I tried to blag the Police but no avail, I thought there's a back way in, so I drove round the back, I thought this is the street, but it was No Entry, well it didn't apply to me, it was a dead end and very narrow, but the road I wanted was the next one up. So there I am attempting to turn around but aware that a Police Officer is approaching, the next thing the PC knocked on my window and said "Sir, are you aware that you are in a one way street?"

I did own up to it, and tried to impress him, with the words that I was on a Home Office Contract, he replied with a very hint of sarcasm, "Well Sir, when you have finished your ten point turn, make your way over to me," pointing at some other place, adding that he was on duty at this point, the question you are wondering is: did I report to him, well would you have? I know I didn't.

Another job worth mentioning was at the Inland Revenue, West Derby (Liverpool) the offices had had new ceilings fitted, so everything in the office had been covered up with plastic sheeting. In an attempt to remove the sheeting, I failed to notice that part of it was attached to a tall filing cabinet, crash; it came over, spilling all its contents all over the floor it's contents, which were micro-cassettes, (I guess that they were claimants statements), they may have been in alphabetical order, well that's before my slight accident. It would have taken me several hours to put them back into the correct sequence as there was that many, so I just loaded them back in any old order, and someone would have had a major job one day. Let's leave Liverpool now and travel to Bolton.

We were working at the offices of United Utilities, and having our morning break, when the fire alarm went off, everyone had to vacate the site, and stand outside in the cold, why mention this I hear you ask? Well, I had been using a specialised steam cleaner, not the pressure washer type, it was light weight and used in the main, in kitchens for sterilising. On this occasion I was using it on the walls, when the water in the machine wanted replenishing, steam shot out and the pressure valve lifted, this could, if left unattended, cause a build up of steam, as I've said we were on our break, and no one could remember if the machine had been switched off. I had visions of facing financial penalties, especially when the fire brigade arrived, all three engines, when the announcement came, " False alarm," I couldn't describe the relief.

Somewhere in the above time frame I was driving my car which was a Fiat Ulysses, which had been purchased on a lease contract, when I went through a Police radar trap, too late, I saw the Policewoman point the speed gun at me. I was doing about forty in a built up area, but because it was a lease car, the summons took ages to arrive. In the meantime Big

Andy had been breathalysed for the second time, which meant when he appeared in court he would receive an automatic three year ban, so we agreed that Andy was driving, sure enough when the summons finally arrived, they could only issue a fine, as he was already banned. The irony of it came much later, after he had served half of his ban, he appealed and got his licence back, complete with an endorsement for speeding!

Now this tale is in today's climate is not, as they say politically correct, but hey ho here goes, I was doing a job for Mansells at Blackburn; it was actually a refurbishment of a labour exchange. We were engaged for not only the industrial cleaning but to sand down the new laminated flooring and we were there for about a month. I had noticed that the young security guard (Asian) seemed to take pleasure of winding up several different tradesmen with statements that he had been out with these white girls who liked the colour of his skin, etc. Anyway, this particular day he decided to have a go at me, it started off with a quiz, "Who was the most famous boxer in the world?" my answer "Cassius Clay," followed by his comment, "And he's Brown," then it was "Who's the greatest Basketball Player in the world?" my answer "Don't know," comment's "And he's brown," and the questions went on, all sportsmen, all the same comment "And he's brown." I thought well he's started it, I'll finish it, so I said "Hang on in there, answer me this, what colour is a white man's shit?" (I could have said muck but I didn't) from that day on, I was his best friend, at lunch time he'd come and ask if we wanted anything from the Chip Shop, we all laughed because by now we all knew what his punch line would be "Any Brown Sauce?"

The next two incidents that happened with Mancells sealed my fate with them. The first incident was me, I was working on the refurbishment of Canada House, when I came off my ladders, causing me to suffer two broken ribs. This had to go into the accident book, which, and this of course is my own opinion, Mancells did not like, as any accidents are taken seriously. The second put the top hat on it, and this was a job I nearly refused, thinking that the job was in Cornwall, I wasn't aware that there was also a Liscard in Liverpool, and it's a pity I didn't refuse it. Again it was a Labour Exchange refurbishment job, and not only entailed industrial cleaning in the building, but I had to engage sub-contractors, abseiler's for the exterior of the building.

It was one of those jobs that I had to supply two teams of men, I worked the day shift, and a friend, Martin, who was actually the commercial manager at Keele Services, worked the night shift. Martin was actually on holiday at the time, his team consisted of two others, and the abseilers were under my control, we completed the job on time and within budget, and I thought all had gone well. However we were in fact what turned out to be our last job, it was at Wrexham on a hospital job. When I had a phone call from the Liscard job's site manager, enquiring about the abseilers that I used, asking were they hired from your area, Stoke? "No", I said "I'd hired a local firm, in fact Wallasey", I asked of course "Why?" the answer staggered me, someone from Stoke had stolen a Mobile Phone from one of the offices, and wait for it, it actually belonged to the Benefit Fraud Squad, they had put a tracer on the calls and it had been used in the Stoke area. I promised immediate action, and quickly found out who the culprits were, I wanted them prosecuted but the Benefit office didn't, as long as they were reimbursed for the cost of the calls, which was about two hundred and thirty pound's. I paid it, but even though Mansells thanked me for the way I handled the situation, I was never offered the opportunity to quote for their work again.

The job situation at Keele Services changed, firstly, they sold out to Granada, who then purchased a new sewage pumping system that did not require daily maintenance. The light inspections were also dropped, I still had the cleaning contract, but then Granada sold the site to Welcome Break, the Area Manager Brian, moved on, and he actually took another position with Granada. He kept in touch with me and routinely offered me work at other Granada sites, which had been re-branded as Moto, this led me into other works areas, such as tiling, industrial painting, deep cleaning and anything else he wanted doing.

The situation at Keele changed somewhat dramatically when another Manager came in, who suggested that I should choose between Welcome Break and Moto, so I decided to stick with Brian at Moto. Shortly after this he became the Managing Director of all the sites in the UK, so I had made the right move. Before we leave Keele I'll tell you another couple of tales, the first one involved the tiling of one of the restaurant's walls. I had a couple of friends doing the job, Derek and Arthur, as the job was nearing completion, Brian came along to inspect it, the expression on his face was priceless, unknown to Brian, Derek only had one eye, and he was not aware that adhesive was splattered all over one of the lens on his glasses.

Another incident involved travellers, a convoy of caravans appeared on the southbound car park, and seemed to be settling down. On the second night, the then manager, Sargie, rang me, in a panic, I arranged for a couple of Road Sweeper Machines to arrive at 3 am, and to spend at least three hours sweeping and empting the car park bins, and to make as much noise as possible. I also approached a couple of regular truckers that I knew, offered them a free breakfast in exchange for them to park close to the caravans, yes, they had refrigerated containers, very noisy, the caravans disappeared! Talking about the car park bins reminds me of one of my staff at Keele;

Big Andy, Andy always had his eye on making a fast buck, from collecting discarded porn magazines, yes, there was always a plentiful supply of these, especially on the lorry park, to whatever else he could lay his hands on. As an example he saw a lorry driver dumping something into the carpark bins, it turned out to be very large packets of cheese for the catering trade, and was out of date. I don't think that they had hit the bottom of the bins, before they were in Andy's grasp, labels off, and sold on, but he wasn't so lucky with his next find, again, he saw a lorry driver pull up, and discard a package into a bin, Andy's there in a flash, hands in the bin, it was still warm, but this time nothing saleable, it was a dead dog.

Then there was the occasion of the Fruit Flies, it was in the KFC and related to the drink dispensers, Coke, Orange and other fizzy drinks, anyway, they had the invasion of fruit flies, and I had the job of cleaning and getting rid of the nuisance. It proved to be a mammoth task, on this occasion I used as help an outside contractor, Terry, an odd job man, who in his words, "Was an expert in every field," he must have been correct, because you certainly couldn't tell him anything, anyway, I bought Terry in on the second day. On the previous day we had cleaned the machine lines, using a very strong acid, in fact it was the strongest acid based product you could buy, and don't forget I was in the trade.

It had to be used very carefully, as I've said Terry was involved on day two, this was on the drains. The floor was impregnated with acid from the previous day, and you could feel the heat retained in the floor tiles, to combat this I used cardboard boxes to kneel/sit on, several times I had to tell Terry to use the cardboard, but as I've already said, you couldn't tell him anything. The following day, he telephoned me saying "He wouldn't be working with me again, as he had been at the Accident Unit half the night, suffering with burns to his backside" he also claimed that "He'd had to have skin grafts."

The last tale about Keele, honestly, in a conversation with their commercial manager Martin, I suggested siting an Ice Cream Van on the car park. I would pay them a percentage of the takings, Martin thought it was a good idea, so I bought one, unfortunately I had jumped the gun, Brian said "No" so big Andy became an ice cream man!

Then there was the time I bought three containers of Gift Ware, it had come out of the Channel Islands, and it was mainly brass ware, but also glass, ornamental swords, etc. I lost a lot of money on this deal, but that's life, what I'm coming to was, one Saturday morning at about 8 am, I was at home when I had visit from the Police, "Was I such a body?" can't quite remember the name they used but it was similar to mine, let's say, Bill Stanier, but is was me they were after, they claimed to have information that I was handling stolen property. They said that they didn't have a search warrant, but they could soon get one, I said "Please yourself, have a look round, I don't know what you are on about," so they searched the house, the garage, the loft even Tina's bedroom. They asked if I had any other premises, I of course said "Yes, I have an industrial unit at Stone," so off to Stone we went, now bear in mind they made out that they claimed to have no knowledge of the unit, they set off from my house in about three cars, with me following in my car, but I knew the shortcuts and arrived there first. As I went to open the unit, I found another detective already there, who asked me if, "I was Bill Stanier?" by this time the others had arrived and I overheard some comments about my correct name.

After another detailed search they admitted defeat, I asked what it was all about, but only got half hearted excuses. I did admit to them that on my way to the unit I was a little apprehensive regarding the gift ware, as there was a large assortment of daggers and swords, but my fears were groundless. At a later date I did find out, it was an ex-boyfriend of Tina's, who had tipped the police off that I had a quantity of stolen power wash machines, and I can honestly say with my hand on my heart that it was a lie.

But I had had a close shave, because another friend of mine was dealing in contraband booze, and asked me if I was interested in bottles of whisky & brandy, at five pound's a bottle. I declined the offer because in my opinion it wasn't worth the hassle, the most you could make was a pound a bottle, after all it was only cheap stuff, Tesco were selling a similar whisky for seven pound's fifty. However talking to another contact he said he wanted ten cases, five of each, and he would see me on the Friday with the money, and collect later. I ordered the ten cases, but being as he hadn't coughed up, I thought I'm not putting three hundred pound's of my money up for no profit, which was just as well, it would have taken some explaining to the Police!

So I moved on, I was still doing Motorway Service area work, Tip Top Chemicals, was not doing as well as I expected or as the sales team had promised, we were just turning money over. Two things happened the first was that ANC the parcel firm cancelled their contract with me, I was offered the option to re-tender but I had no intention of doing it for silly money, so that was a major loss, and the second thing I had a lawsuit imminent, one of my sales force, (Big Andy) had allegedly placed an order for a chemical from a firm in Manchester, this in my opinion would have been a loss making product. Lawyers were involved, my solicitor interviewed Big Andy, and he was not impressed by his attitude and advised me that it was his impression that he would not be a reliable witness under cross examination, so I put Mapleshore Ltd, trading as Tip Top Chemicals into administration, with immediate effect.

The Motorway Service area work, came under my other company TWS Supplies Ltd. The trouble with the motorway service areas was that we could go a couple of months doing nothing, then bang three to five days non-stop working anywhere in the country, so what could I do to fill in on the spare days? I leased a garage in Longton, and started a fresh venture.

Job 42 Self-drive Van hire; Value Van Hire & Job 43 Second Hand Car Sales,

I gave the Van Hire Twelve months to be a success, and whilst in some quarters it did quite well. I quickly realised that to be successful I would have to invest more money, and I didn't think it was worth the risk. There was never any happy medium; we were either quiet or busy. I had a Sprinter Van, a 308 and 408 van, one seven and half ton box van with tail lift, and a seven and half curtainsider, plus a LWB pick up truck, all Mercedes. A new law was being implemented that stipulated that seven and half ton vehicles could only be hired out to holders of operating licences, which was not the market I was targeting.

I wanted the home removals etc., also Customs & Excise were clamping down on Booze trips. Even though customers when hiring our vans were not allowed to take the vehicles out of the country, and signed to this effect, (I suspected in some cases that in fact they were used for this purpose), the vehicle would still be impounded and not released, the fact that we could prove that we were blameless meant nothing. So coupled with the car sales, and even though I had obtained my Consumers Credit Licence for five years, issued by the Office of Fair Trading, I considered it was not worth the hassle.

I had cars broken into, thieves cutting the fuel lines to empty the petrol tanks, we even had a car stolen from our premises in Longton, which was found abandoned in Bentilee, which was less than two miles away. The police would not allow us to collect it from where it had been found, we had to go to the authorised recovery firm and pay a hundred and twenty four pound's. I worked out that if we didn't turn around a sale car in three weeks we would lose money on it, so after the twelve months I closed it down.

Job 44, Industrial Painter

I was still doing work on the Motorways, which I should add, had never gone away, in fact it had started to get busy and soon we were travelling all over the country again working on various Moto sites. A couple of times a year I would have to do a job that entailed visiting every site in the country, by country I mean England, Wales & Scotland. If my memory serves me right, they had forty two sites which included two in Wales and two in Scotland. This job could not be sub-contracted out, it had be yours truly, Mike my right hand man usually accompanied me. If we left home early on a Monday morning, and worked a twelve to fourteen hour day, and averaged one hour per site, it would take us nine days to complete. One such job entailed me checking that each site had complied with head offices instructions to paint a wall yellow, and then we had to attach the relevant health and safety notices on it, if a site had not painted the said wall, my instructions were to fine them five hundred pound's, and surprisingly I did fine about three sites.

When I arrived at Kinross in Scotland obviously they were expecting me, for there hanging on the yellow wall was a big sheet of cardboard saying, 'Bill Stanton's walls don't touch!' The sites that failed my inspections had to be revisited at a later date to check that they had indeed painted them. One such site, still failed, the managers argument to me was that the wall was yellow, when in my opinion it was Magnolia, all I know was I didn't go back for a third visit. The only other problem I encountered on this job, was at Woolley Edge Services, no way could we drill the walls in the staff room, we were not aware that it was the former Electric Sub Station, the walls were lead lined, it was only after several drill bits later that we found out, believe me No Nails is a good product!

Another one of these all site jobs Mike and I were involved in, was fitting a new type of Toilet Seat Wipe Dispenser in the toilets, both ladies and gents, we also had to put up signs with the instructions, however, as Moto found out to their cost, people didn't read the notices, they were being used as hand wipes! Another job that comes to mind was the Burger King job, this was at the time that Burger King were doing a promotion that involved giving away free gifts with children's meals. The gifts were items such as watches, games etc., my job was to visit every site in the country in my seven & half ton van, re-distributing the toy's around. Some sites had used more of certain things and were short of others etc., anyway, I'm sure you've got the picture.

Linda came with me and we started off travelling on the North route, out via Knutsford, Birch, Lancaster, working our way to Scotland, stopping overnight at Travel Lodges. Then from Scotland southbound via Newcastle on Tyne, all went well until we hit the Luton area. It was Wimbledon Tennis

Championship time, and we could not get accommodation anywhere, I even involved the girls at Moto Headquarters, which was at Toddington, no luck, there was simply ' No room at the Inn,' I drove off route around Bedford, Luton etc., eventually we ended up at South Minns on the M25, the opposition, Welcome Break, still no luck. So it was kip in the back time, I arranged the boxes so that Linda could lie flat, but no such luck for me, mine were up and down, all different sizes and shapes, but I've always said that I could sleep on a clothes line, now's the time to prove it. So we both settled down for the night.

The first interruption we encountered was a driver urinating at the back of our truck, a quick shout of hoy, which must have made him dribble down his legs, was met with a few mumbles of "Sorry mate." Then remember its Wimbledon time, so it must have been June, the heavens opened, have you ever lay there listening to thunder and then hailstones bouncing off a Perspex roof? But then because of the position I was lying in, I got cramp in my leg, and couldn't get up. To try and get warm, I'd put both my arms into the legs of my spare pair of trousers, which gave us both the giggles, at that we gave up, we jumped out into the pool of urine and went to have a cup of tea, but not before removing the parking ticket I had attracted, which I may add I never paid.

So off we went doing the southern area, as far as Brighton (Peas Pottage) across via the M4 to Heston (Heathrow) to Exeter then to South Wales, where we had arranged to meet our youngest daughter Tina, who was studying at Swansea University. The plan was to have a meal with her, but Linda baled out and stayed with Tina, leaving me to carry on with the rest of the journey. Another 'all sites job' that entailed using my truck, was to take away from each site all their surplus stock from the shops, and to then find a buyer for it. It was not the best of jobs in such, as each site had different ideas as to what to throw out, i.e. some even included old magazines, which were perhaps several years old, and weighed heavy. So say you did the first five sites and they disposed of gift ware, that was light in weight, then you get to the sixth site and their surplus stock was heavy, it proved very difficult to stack.

As soon as the truck was loaded full, I returned to unload into the pre-arranged buyer, my mate Mario's warehouse, and then start again. I did about five journeys, and raised ten thousand pound's, but what proved a nice earner for me was that it was the time that cigarettes could only be sold that displayed 'Health Warning Signs,' all old stock had to be destroyed, now I don't smoke, never have and never will, but I knew plenty of people that did.

The thing about working at these different sites, was we never knew what we would be doing next, one job would be painting, and I seemed to get a lot of these jobs, even though in truth I can't paint and don't even like painting, but painting jobs would always be different site to site. At Birch Services on the M62, we had to paint every bedroom in the Travel Lodges, both sides of the Motorway, about ninety bedrooms. I would take a team of about eight men, and set the job up.

We would aim for doing eight rooms a day, bear in mind that the rooms were in use. I would detail one man to do the masking out and cover the exposed areas of carpet, furniture, beds TV etc., as soon as he had done that another team men would start painting the ceilings, then the next team would do the walls, and so on. Once I had set this up, all I had to do was keep my eye on them, anyway, on this particular morning I was sitting (honest) in one of the bedrooms with one of the chambermaid's having a cup of tea, when her mobile phone rang, it was her husband, she was chatting away with him, and as she was coming to the end of the conversation, I shouted, "Love You", he enquired "Who's that?" her reply was "It's only Bill the painter," now bear in mind he knows where she works and what it entails, you would never guess the question he asked her? "Is he a Man City supporter?" I whispered to her, "Whatever you do don't tell him I'm from Stoke."

Another time at Birch we were doing a major cleanup that involved day and night work. I was in charge of the days and Big Andy nights. Days was cleaning whilst nights was painting. The M62 is described as a commuter route, which means it was only busy in the day, night time was very quiet. Andy's brief this night was to paint the interior of the bridge that connected the two sites. The East bound side was open for eating and shop facilities, West bound was toilets only, at about one or two in the morning they decided to take a break, leaving the equipment and paint in situ, on their return paint had been thrown all over the place, the rest of the night was spent cleaning up the mess. Before I leave Birch I must tell you about the Commonwealth Games, for the duration of the games which was eleven days, I was stationed there. For the first six days Mike was with me, and then his son, Simon came, anyway each day we were given different tasks, on this particular day, I rang Linda telling her I was on gardening duties, she laughed as she knew I couldn't tell a weed from a flower, I told her "No problem, if it isn't a Carnation it comes out."

Well, months later Linda and I were at Birch with the deputy manager, John, and as we walked over to the Travel Lodge I nudged Linda and pointed out the bare flower beds, John turned round and saw us looking at the beds, and commented, "What do think Bill someone had stolen the plants!" Birch

Services gave me the hardest graft ever. My brief was to utilize part of the West Bound car park, and make a Coach Park. The job sounded simple, it was decided that the best way of doing it, would to be insert an island close to the entrance of the car park, coming out forty feet so that coaches could reverse into the bays. This I would achieve by way of using line markings and signage, what I didn't know until I started the job, that kerb stones have as much buried as is showing, we had to dig out two channels for the kerb stones. I had a team of six men on this; I hired three kangoo hammers, which were going non stop.

The car park surface on these service areas are extra strengthened, and were a nightmare to dig up. If I had known what I knew after, I would have hired JCB's, we were all well and truly shattered by the time we had finished it. For the final touches I hired a firm from Blackpool to do the lane marking. Working at Thurrock Services on the M25, for those who don't know where this is, it's just before the Queen Elizabeth Bridge, in Kent, that's going towards Dover, or coming back it's just after the Dartford Tunnel. The job there was painting the site, I never realised just how high up it was. I was working outside painting the railing when the wind blew the paint out of my tray! Whilst I'm talking about working down south, I must tell you about Heston Services, on the M4, this site is the nearest to Heathrow. For a change we weren't painting, we were regrouting the toilets, it was a Saturday night, which was the quietest night of the week.

I had two teams, one in the Ladies and the other doing the Gents. We shut the Ladies, they could use the disabled, but the Gents we couldn't. As you can imagine we created a lot of white powder, which tended to get carried out on their shoes. This next bit I can't tell without swearing, but that's how it happened, so here goes, as the night went on we were aware that an increasing numbers of foreign lorry drivers were in and out, the lorry park was full of parked up lorries from in the main, Poland and Bulgaria, and again we were aware that they were intoxicated. I'd had a bit of banter with them in broken English, but they were a nuisance, as every trip to the toilet meant they had to walk through the dust we had created, resulting in a white trail of powder on the floor. I was in the Ladies, when Mike came to me complaining that one of them, had started to pick up the men's tools, I shot round and confronted the culprit, putting my face in his face, and saying in my best broken English, "You speakah the English", he replied, "I no speakah the English", so I then said, "Why don't you fukkee off," his reply had us in hysterics, "I no money for coffee."

It was from this job that we were travelling home about 4am on the Sunday morning, I was doing about ninety miles an hour on the M1, half asleep, when a Police car drew along side us, the officer in the passenger seat, turned and faced me, had a good look at me, and then just accelerated away, it must have been my lucky night. Another time just a few miles from Heston still on the M4 we were doing a major paint job at Reading Services on both sides of the motorway. We were there for about a week, come the Sunday, I have never seen as many people, there was coach load, after coach load of people, all travelling to London to demonstrate against the ban on 'Fox Hunting,' and according to my friendly Google site it was September 22nd, 2002.

Google claim that over four hundred thousand people turned out. I think half of them stopped at Reading Services. It was that bad, we had to stop work, we were working on ladders and steps, and the shear volume of bodies made it unsafe, in fact the shop on the inward journey broke all records, it took ten thousand pound's in one shift! A little closer to home, Tamworth services on the M42, this was another major cleaning job; I seem to remember they were having a visit from the local MP, so the site had to look pristine, about 3am we couldn't gain access to gain either an electric supply or water, I can't really remember which. What I can remember was the area I needed to get into was alarmed, and the night staff didn't have the code, so I had to ring the designated site manager for it, however I still couldn't gain access, it could have been a wrong code, so rather than bother the sleeping manager, I managed to get round the problem.

The following day, I received a phone call from the sites Area General Manager, asking me about the area that I had proposed working from, I pointed out that we in fact had not been able to gain access, but why the questions, the reply shocked me. It had caught fire, and caused considerable damage, thank goodness I didn't gain entry. Talking about fire, we had a job on at Grantham Services, it was over two nights, and the job actually was initially a deep clean. The kitchen tiles were a dirty grey colour, however, on a closer inspection the tiles had all been painted and had discoloured, so in the allocated time we could not strip all the old paint off and then clean the tiles, plus all the kitchen ovens, sinks etc had to be cleaned, so it was down to B & Q for washable emulsion paint in large quantity's. We worked all night until 6 the next morning, after enjoying a cooked breakfast, we all went to our pre-booked bedrooms on the sites Travel Lodge. I was sharing with Big Andy, well, I've never heard anybody snore like him, if he wasn't snoring he was snorting, if he wasn't snorting he was mumbling. I tried to cut out the noise with the pillows over my head, but no avail, so I gave up.

Next door to the service area, was one of those discount warehouses, so I went for a stroll in there. A couple of hours later, my mobile rang, it was Andy, enquiring "Where was I?" he sounded relieved when I told him, apparently there had been a fire alarm, the fire brigade had attended, all the guests had to vacate the lodge, but I couldn't be accounted for, some one had discarded a cigarette into a rubbish bin in of the bathrooms, and no it wasn't one of my men, thank goodness.

As I've stated before we never knew what the next job would be or entail, take Forton Services, now known as Lancaster. I had an urgent call, a young man had attempted suicide in one of the Travel Lodges bedrooms, and the room had been sealed off. On entering the room I found a one litre bottle of Vodka that was nearly empty and a broken glass, which I assumed he had used to cut his wrist, he must have sat on the edge of the bed letting the blood drain into a waste bin; there was blood all over the place. How he was discovered was, that as his blood slowly drained away, and the effects of the Vodka took hold on his body, he had become cold and disoriented, and he was found wandering the Lodges corridors with a duvet wrapped around him. A member of staff approached him, and the Police were called, it was very sad, but what made our job worse, was that the bedrooms heating was on at full blast and the window left open, the room was overlooking farmland, and was full of flies.

When I received the call I rang Mike and he agreed to come with me, when I went to pick him up, his son, Simon asked if he could come as well, claiming that he had worked in a slaughterhouse, so the blood wouldn't bother him. We entered the room, which had a foul smell, and quickly got to work, Mike got the Wet & Dry vacuum out and was sucking up the blood from the carpet, I was sponging down the furniture and told Simon to empty the waste bin that had contained his blood into the toilet, well the blood had congealed and solidified, and took some getting out of the bin. I went into the bathroom to see what the problem was just as the lot went plop, and Simon went as white as a ghost.

It was at this site on much earlier occasion that I had encountered a problem with a local farmer. My instructions had been to repair and replace fencing where it was I deemed necessary. I was walking around the field looking at what materials would be required when this bloke on a quad bike appeared, when I say bloke I should say 'Angry Bloke.' "What the **** hell did I think I was doing?" he asked, I explained that I had been given instructions to make the fence good, as the Management were worried about the sheep straying onto the motorway. It soon became apparent that the fence was not on land belonging to the Motorway Service Area, the farmer demanded that the manager meet him, I explained that it was a situation that was of benefit to him, and that in fact the site was going through the motions of appointing a new manager, anyway he calmed down, and we made safe certain areas, but didn't put any new fencing in.

Every so often Brian (M.D.) or his secretary would meet me with a new project, and put their ideas to me, and I would have to come up with the end product. The ones that come to mind offhand were a children's play area which was to have tables with pictures of Moto Mouse engraved/embossed into the tabletops, this was trialled at Exeter, and although it was well received there it was not followed up at other sites. On another occasion Brian had been to America, and was impressed with their point of sale in their refrigerated displays, so with the help of a local refrigeration company I had a couple of conversions done, using fine crushed ice, and sectioned off display areas, these were put in at Stafford and Birch. But the one that turned out to be a nightmare of a job, was again the result of an American visit, in principal it was straight forward, my brief was to produce a tabletop receptacle so that the diners could place their rubbish in.

It was to coincide with the withdrawal of tea pots and the introduction of Tea Bags and Mugs, one had to sit on each table on every site, so as you can imagine there was a few thousand to be manufactured. I had a prototype made that met with his approval, it had a circular base with the words

"Trash" cut out, and a large ring of metal that a circular container would fit in, that could easily be emptied. The stands were approved and were manufactured locally, on completion I had them sandblasted and plastic coated, I bought as a demo, a flower pot that could serve as model for the size which were to fit inside the stand to allow for easy emptying. My intention was that the end product was to be a stainless steel bowl, I even sent off to China one of the flower pots as a guide for measurement and size, and for costing. However, I was over ruled, and the plant pots were deemed as suitable, the supplier of these pots were IKEA, and the agreement was that I would deliver the stands to the sites. Now this is where the nightmare started, at the last minute it was discovered that IKEA would not deliver to the sites, only to Moto's head office at Toddington, so yours truly left home one morning at 6 am, and made his way to Toddington, arriving at 9 am, wait around until about 11 am, help unload IKEA'S van, and try and sort out a plan of action.

There was no way I had room for all the pots and my stands, so I loaded up my van to deliver to all points South East of Toddington. This would have been about a 2pm departure, first call Thurrock, then all the southern sites and then back to Toddington. This bought me to lunch time on the following day, I had contacted Mike to hire a van and meet me at Toddington, he arrived shortly after, where we loaded his van up for Bristol, Cardiff and Swansea, then up the M5 for the Midlands as far as Stafford. It should be noted that Mike was unwell, but rather than let me down, he got one of his son's to drive and he navigated, that is what I call a true friend and employee.

I loaded up for the rest of the country, starting with Cherwell Valley, then doing the rest of the sites as far as Scotland etc, I arrived at Grantham at 3am the next morning, that's forty five hours later, staying in the Travel Lodge there, had breakfast and left at 7 am that's four hours rest and recuperation.

Then off to Blyth and the rest finally finishing at Knutsford some nineteen hours later, but mission completed, the whole job was completed in four days, four days at twenty four hours per day = ninety six hours, I had worked sixty four of them, had the pots been delivered to Stoke it would have made the job a lot easier. I had that many breakages I was worried that I would not have sufficient pots. I had allowed an extra ten per site, twenty for twin sided sites, as I got towards the end of the journey I was giving loads of extras away and still finished with about a hundred surpluses, so you can see why I called it a nightmare! As a point of interest, I did have an enquiry about supplying these to an Army Regiment, but nothing came of it.

Before we leave Motorway services areas, let me tell you about a couple of incidents at Keele Services, firstly the time

Linda and I was invited to the Keele Managers Christmas
Party held at an Hotel in Shrewsbury, Martin, their Commercial
Manager invited me, and pointed out that it was a 'Black tie'
do. Now, I'm more knowledgeable in the world of social
etiquette, but back then a black tie to me meant a black tie not
a 'dickie bow', yep, I stood out like a prize idiot, good job I'm
thick skinned and not easily embarrassed. The other story,
well this I was not directly involved in, but it's worth repeating.

Keele was in the process of having the Gents toilets converted
to automatic flushes. On the initial installation a couple of
teething problems were encountered, and I remember a rather
angry truck driver demanded to see the duty manager, who on
this occasion happened to be female, but it was the way that
he presented the problem that amused me, his words were "If
you're going to install arse washing facilities, can we at least
have warm water."

Around about 1995 on holiday in Turkey I met a guy we will
call Mr.K. who was from our area, and we hit it off
straightaway. It turned out that he had at one time applied for
a job at Tip Top Chemicals, as a sales representative, I hadn't
followed it up because in my opinion he was too qualified,
anyway, he was working at a well known gas company, as
their Export Manager, and we started up a company between
us, called KAZ International, which me led to:-

Job 45 ADR Driver,

This entailed transporting gas to various locations around the UK; it meant Big Andy and myself, going on a course to obtain our ADR licences. It's now education time, ADR is an acronym taken from the French language, Accord European Relatif au Transport International des Marchandises Dangerouses par Route, impressed? What it meant was that I and Andy were now licensed to carry dangerous/hazard goods. Before I diverse let me tell about a couple of jobs on this ADR, I was hired to take several types of gas cylinders to Harrogate. You are required to know what the contents are in cases of emergencies. On this particular morning as the saying goes, I felt it in my water that I was going to get stopped, and lo and behold I was. Feeling pleased with myself, I was ready for any question that might be put to me, but there were none, it was just a weighbridge stop. The enforcement officer said "Pull over to the side after the weigh in," he came back to me with a very stern look, and informed me, "That I was over weight on my rear axle, by 9.4%, (long pause) and the law states that you are allowed 10%", he then smiled.

I called him a name, but only in fun, he did explain to me that I was in fact lucky that the law had been recently amended to allow this 10%, before it would have had to go to the Traffic Commissioners for their consideration. Then there was the job to take six bottles of Helium Gas to Bordeaux in the South of France. It was to be used to blow up balloons in a Rugby cup match, Harlequins verses Bordeaux. I covered over two thousand miles in four days. As gas leaves a residue it had to be deck cargo both ways. K. came with me, and we bought our wives a present back. K bought his wife a sexy negligee I bought Linda a plastic covered tablecloth, (see I'm still the romantic). We still use the table cloth, bet K's wife isn't wearing the negligee!

Another job that K and I undertook, was to take a television producers house contents from Llandudno to Narbonne, in the South of France, this was going to be a round journey of over two thousand miles. For the job we hired two self-drive 7.5 ton vans, we journeyed down to Portsmouth for the sailing to Caen arriving in France at about ten in the evening. We arrived there with empty fuel tanks, because it was common knowledge that the price of fuel in France was considerably less than here. What we didn't know was, that the service stations close at ten, and the ones that were open were self-service, ok I know you're thinking, self service no problem, but the problem was that the pumps wouldn't accept our English credit/debit cards, so we carried on as far as we dared, before settling down in a lay-by,. We even tried to buy some from lorry drivers, who of course couldn't speak English, and we couldn't speak French. Eventually we did manage to make one lorry driver understand, but unfortunately we could only manage to siphon a gallon out of his tank.

So it was a cold night spent trying to sleep in our cabs, eventually day break came, and we did find a petrol station in an isolated village, so again it was settle down in the cab, and wait for opening. We journeyed through the beautiful French countryside eventually arriving in Narbonne late afternoon on the second day. We had stayed overnight in the Vichy area, where I sampled the best pint of draught 1664 lager I had ever tasted, it was pure nectar. After unloading, we stayed the night in a very charming Chateau, which our customers from Llandudno had purchased, early the next morning saw us setting of once again, but not before we had called at a local supermarket, and stocked up with the local wines.

I can't actually recall where the overnight stay was on the return journey, however I do remember driving off the ferry in Portsmouth just before ten in the evening, stopping once for fuel, and arriving home at just after one the morning. I jumped out of the cab, clutching my two bottles of duty free Jack Daniels, tripped on the kerb, and went headfirst into my rose bushes, my ears caught the brunt of the fall, and as you can imagine the blood was flowing, but the duty free was ok! Linda had to put a towel over my head to staunch the blood, when I got out of bed; there was imprint of thorns of where I had lain.

Let's talk about Kaz International, on paper it looked good, and business was good, however what we were doing was to be truthful, not legal, I'll not tell you how or why, just believe me. K had several contacts and at this stage we were very good friends, both in business and in our social lives. We even went on a cruise with them, and went on a business trip/holiday to Hong Kong, which both Linda and I enjoyed the sights there, however it was on this trip that doubts in K began to merge. He claimed to be an expert in export and import, and whilst in Hong Kong, negotiated the shipment of quality furniture from the Far East, and fed me a pack of lies as to their importation.

In fact as I found out later, no such furniture ever reached these shores, he returned to Hong Kong at a later date, and came back with wonderful tales of importing Aluminium Barrels. Which of course never happened, before we leave Hong Kong let me tell you about the time we decided to take a ride on the local tram, we ended up at the terminus somewhere, as we crossed over the track, we noticed this building marked Market. As we entered the building I was encountered a stall selling model buses, PMT Hanley-Barlaston, Hanley-Lichfield, there was also Stevenson's of Uttoxeter double decker's proudly displayed for sale.

In the meantime for the occasion of his wife's birthday, we went over to France on a Booze run, and to cut a long story short, on the return journey we were pulled over by the Police. This was on the M6, not far from Corley Services, after questioning at the roadside the Police Officer said, "Sir I must stress that neither you, or your friend are under arrest, however your vehicle is impounded until the customs have cleared it." This comment was met by me, as per usual making a sarcastic comment of, "Would the Police Officer like me to have a lie down on the motorway hard shoulder while we wait?" (It was pouring down with rain) which was met by the perfect calm, reassuring tone of the officer replying "Well if Sir would prefer, they had an office at the nearby service area, would I drive the vehicle there". Really it left me with no option but to agree. We had to sit in an office whilst they got clearance, during this time K sat with his head in his hands, he had lost it big time.

Now as I've said our business was not legal, I realised that if it came under scrutiny he would go to pieces, so shortly after this I pulled out of the company. In response to his question of why, I answered him truthfully, "That I had in the past been involved in criminal activities, we were pushing our luck and I wanted out." he never did believe me, but that's up to him. In some ways he was very amateurish, even when he gave me the forms to sign to say that I was resigning as Company

Secretary, he folded it up, thinking that I could not see that in fact I was signing my shares away, but I wasn't bothered. I wanted out, and I never did receive any of the considerable monies in the account.

Job 46 Property Maintenance

As I was fast approaching the magical age of retirement, sixty-five, I told Brian I wouldn't be doing anymore work on the Motorways, it had got too much for me, however, K had a retail unit on the Hyde Park Industrial Estate, and I had got to know the sites owner, who offered me odd painting jobs. When I say odd jobs, I had to have a full team working when required, but that came to a untimely end. We had done a massive cleanup on a unit that in its past life had been a Steam Trains workshop. It was a major job, and the owner of the business estate was impressed, in so much that he gave us the job of renovating his own workshop/offices/toilets & showers.

Part way through the project the specification was changed, from lining the shower walls in plastic sheeting to tiles. I did have a problem getting hold of a tiler at short notice, and this did hold the job up, plus another unit was let at short notice, and I had to tie this extra work in. The end result was that we were about two weeks behind schedule. Now I must stress that I had in the past no problem with payment, he always paid prompt on the thirty days, but on these two jobs, no money. I left it to what I considered was a reasonable time, before writing and threatening court action to recover the debt. It was a standard letter, however I had threatened action in the High Court, not the County Court; this was because of the amount involved, which was over five thousand Pounds plus VAT.

On receipt of the letter he did ring me, expressing surprise at the tone of the letter, and went on to explain, that his intention was to delay payment by the amount of days I had run over on the completion of his refurbishment. No allowance had been given for the additional work or the change in specification, but as I pointed out my delay was fourteen days, not coming up to a month. He agreed on this, saying that this was an oversight on his side regarding the payment, he paid the outstanding debt, but no more work came our way. It was on this job that sitting in the mobile café one morning, I read the Daily Mirror, and there was an advert for Agency Bus Drivers, ten pound's an hour, this was 2004, PSV drivers in our area were on less than a fiver an hour.

So I rung up and left my details. About a month later I had a phone call asking if I was interested in driving for a North Staffordshire Bus Company, I asked "Where was it, and what pay were they offering", the answer surprised me "Ten pound's an hour and it's at Newcastle," I said "This must be

First Bus," (Formally PMT) they confirmed that it was. I confirmed my interest saying "Yes I'll do it but there could be a problem," and went to explain that this was the depot that ten years ago had previously bought me out, in fact 'to shut me up', the Agency approached the Management at First's depot, and said "They will welcome you back with open arms."

Job 47 Agency Driver

So for the next nine months I worked at First Bus Newcastle Depot, then at Crewe, and I must say that I enjoyed it. At Newcastle I had to do route training, on the routes I had sold to them, mainly Clayton. The biggest struggle I had was with the ticket machines. There was some animosity shown to certain agency drivers but I never experienced any. After about six months I transferred to the Crewe Depot, and ended up doing Monday – Friday on the same route, admittedly it was the last bus in at night, but I was on about five hundred and fifty pound's a week, which in 2005 was a very good wage.

I did have a couple bouts of trouble with drunks, but nothing I couldn't handle, one was on the last bus going through Talke Pits when two youths attempted to get on the bus with bottles in their hands; I said "It's a no go lads, either throw them away or get off," it transpired they only wanted a free ride up the bank, I said "Last chance lads, get shut of the bottles and get your money out, or the next stop will be Kidsgrove," about four miles away. It made no difference, so the doors shut, and away we went, with these two idiots standing at the front of the bus. As I said before I did this run every night, and knew that there would be no one else to pick up.

One of the youths tried to grab the steering wheel, saying "He would knock me out," but this threat didn't seem real, as tears were rolling down his face, maybe due to the fact I was bending his fingers right back. I stopped at Kidsgrove and threw them off. I had chosen Kidsgrove because I knew that by then I would have passed the other last bus going in the direction they had come from.

The other occasion involved Kidsgrove again, but this time I was going the other way, but I was still the last bus. As I drove down Kidsgrove Bank, a fight from a nearby pub spilled out onto the road, and I was faced with this youth, stripped to the waist, gesturing for me to come on, so I did, hitting him with an almighty bang with the side of the bus, and carried on. Further on in the journey, as one of the regulars was getting off, I asked him if he'd seen the incident, he had, and the last he'd seen was the youth being carried away by his mates. So on my way home I called at Kidsgrove Police Station, which I knew would be unmanned and spoke by telephone to Central Control, explaining that I had witnessed a fight and had they any record of it. The answer was "No", so that was a relief; you can't report something that never happened can you?

On this route one afternoon, I was booking fares in Hanley Bus Station, when a lady came up to me complaining that a male was smoking. I went to him, and told him "No smoking," he mumbled something and put his fag out. He had booked to Tunstall, on arrival in Tunstall I looked in my mirror, he was asleep, I looked again in Kidsgrove, Talke Pits and Chesterton, still asleep, when we got to Newcastle I went to him and shook him saying "Come on pal Tunstall," off he went, he was high on something.

As I've already said I was approaching sixty five, two weeks before my birthday, I told the agency I would be finishing. They sent a manager from London to try and make me change my mind, I explained that "I started work on my fifteenth birthday and I was finishing on my sixty-fifth." Six months later they were still ringing me up offering me work in Bristol, Manchester, London – Stanstead express, even Dublin.

So here I am retired, yes, no chance.

Job 48 Van Driver. National Milk Records, Meaford Power Station

This was a part time position; the mileage you covered was amazing. The job entailed collecting samples, mainly milk. The vans were insulated, and were a very modern fleet of Mercedes, mainly Sprinters, a couple of Vito's and a 7.5 ton Atego. To illustrate the mileage covered, one Thursday I drove a brand new Sprinter. I had to wait for it to be unloaded from the transporter, it had covered ten miles, by the following Thursday I was on the same run and had the same van, and it had covered three and a half thousand miles in that week!

The first day on the job, I was given my work detail, I thought great, local work. The first collection was from Loggerheads, I picked up the samples and asked if they knew where my next one was, yes, no problem Market Drayton, just down the road. Same procedure, but this time a shake of the head, my next pick up was Caernarfon a hundred miles away, and another couple of pickups in Wales. We used to go as far as Lockerbie in Scotland, and further still was the South East Coast run which took you around Clacton on Sea.

Bearing in mind the daily mileage, I only had one summons for speeding, and that was at Cellarhead! Local unbelievable. I had been stopped once before, it was somewhere in mid Wales, I had been following this car for what seemed like miles, when I spied my chance, foot down, it was at this moment that I saw the Police Officer with his radar gun pointing at me, a quick look in the mirror confirmed it, blue flashing lights, but I was in country lanes, and it was a couple of miles until I spotted a safe place to pull in.

The Police car was following behind but he had turned his blue lights off, I apologised saying "I wasn't being funny but I didn't think it was safe to stop beforehand," he agreed with me, asking "Did I know what speed I was doing when he had clocked me, and did I know what the speed limit was?" I replied "Yes and No, no to what speed I was actually doing, and yes to knowing the speed limit, because I was driving a commercial vehicle, forty mph," he then said, "Well to be honest with you, you're the first van driver I've pulled up, that either knows the law, or admits to it," I had to go to his car where he showed me the radar gun, with my speed recording, sixty three mph. Then he asked "Is it your my own van?" "No, it was National Milk Records," I replied, next question "What are you carrying?" Now this was not me trying to be funny, I had a mental block.

I replied "Milk samples and bulls spunk," the word I was looking for was sperm, but he laughed, and asked me for my drivers licence, date of birth etc. I couldn't produce the insurance, so he started to write out the ticket, he then said, "Look produce the insurance within the specified time, I have to issue you with a ticket, but I am putting down that the reason for stopping you was that you were speeding, however, I am not putting the speed recording down, as I would have to book you. Produce the ticket and you won't hear anything about It." and I didn't. As we parted I explained I was lost, he gave me directions, I said "Well officer I didn't think I'd be saying this, but a Merry Christmas to you and your family."

The job in itself was a well paid job, but because of the areas covered, every day was a long one. Your average start time was at twelve noon, and finish twelve midnight. The bug bear was at the end of your run, all samples had to be delivered to the laboratories in Wolverhampton, which was no problem if you coming that way, but a bind if you had been on the Scottish or Lake District areas. The only perk of the job was that you had a BP agency card to fill up with, so as you can imagine you soon built up a substantial amount of nectar points. If I remember right this would be the year that Tina bought all her Christmas presents from the Nectar catalogue.

I was supposed to work about three days a week, but often more, but then they said part-timers had to work every Saturday and Sunday, I didn't mind occasionally but not every weekend. The only day the vans didn't go out was Christmas day. I was on the Welsh run on a New Years day, the route took me through Llangollen and over the mountains, it had been snowing, and the view was amazing. I remember thinking I was the only vehicle on the road, I hadn't seen any other vehicles for ages. As I climbed up the side of the mountain, I went around a corner, and I was in a traffic jam! All the villagers from around were on their sledges, an amazing sight.

It was in Wales that I decided to quit, well I wasn't happy about the weekend working, and then I had had a front wheel blow out, in the middle of nowhere. I was on a narrow country road, I had no telephone signal, and if there had have been I couldn't pronounce the name of where I was, I managed to change the wheel, but I thought to myself do I really need this?

Job 49 Point of Sale Van Delivery Driver.

Now, I'd known Ivan for years, in fact I used to deal with his dad, Ian Jones. They were based at Etwall in Derbyshire; Ivan bought vans from various auction centres around the country, and then he sold them mainly via E-Bay. He would purchase a van from, say Glasgow auctions, immediately take photographs of it and put it on E-Bay. I have known occasions that the van has been sold before Ivan had taken delivery. The problem was, what was wrong with the van that had been put up for auction? If there was a delay in the vans preparation because of a fault and delay in sorting, Ivan would then offer the customer delivery; this is where I would come in.

I would deliver it anywhere in the Country, and come back on the train, and I really enjoyed it. It was very interesting and I went to some beautiful parts of the Country, but Ivan's knowledge of geography was, to be kind, very poor, as an example "Bill can you deliver one to London tomorrow?" When I went to collect the van I'd look at the post code, it's not London it's Southampton! Ivan's comments, "Well it's down that way!"

It was one of these jobs that I had another brush with law, but this time in my own van. I had a little Vauxhall combo van, and as many other people do, it had a handwritten sign in the back window stating that the van was for sale. I had had a rough day, delivering a Mazda van to Poole in Dorset. I'd had to wait for the van, not an unusual thing, after about twenty miles it developed a faulty injector pipe. The engine was in cab and I was literally eating diesel, Ivan said, "Carry on I'll sort it out with the customer." I was on the M27 just on the outskirts of Southampton. Due to an uphill gradient, I couldn't even reach thirty mph, so as you may imagine it was late when I reached my destination. The customer did eventually accept the motor, but it was about ten at night when I arrived at Derby rail station. Ivan was waiting for me, so it must have been about eleven pm when I was driving home past the Britannia Stadium on the A50, when I spotted the blue flashing lights.

I pulled over, the question was; "Do you know why you have been stopped?" My reply was, "Well officer it could be one of two reasons, number one, I was speeding," the officer replied, "Spot on, do you know the speed limit?" "Yes forty" "Well I've followed you from Blythe Bridge and at times you were nearly doing seventy," I said "Sorry but I've had a really rough day" and told him of the days experiences. He then asked what the number two reason was, I smiled and said, "I thought you may have been interested in buying the vehicle," he laughed and said, in his words, "You've coughed up, watch your speed, and get off home."

Several times on delivery of a van I have collected the purchase price, sometimes cash and sometimes a cheque, and if it was in a sealed envelope I would accept it on trust, however, on this occasion it was an old Audi car, which in itself was unusual. It was to a district in the middle of London, the purchaser was a Foreigner, and he invited me in for a cup of tea, which I gratefully accepted. The deal was a cash transaction of twelve hundred pounds, he handed me the money in a sealed envelope, but on this occasion, I don't know why, I opened it and counted it. It was three hundred pound's short. He said, "It can't be, I've just drawn it out of the bank," I said, "Well we'll count it again," same result, at that he said, "Oh yes, I remember, I'd drawn an additional three hundred pound's from out of an ATM," and pulled the money from his back pocket.

He asked if I was alright finding the tube station, and gave me a route. As I left his place I looked at the route he had given me, and noted that it involved walking through a park, so I thought no, I'll go the other way, it may be longer but safer. This was the only occasion that I'd felt unsafe, even in some of the roughest parts of Glasgow I never felt intimidated.

Take Motherwell the deal was on receipt of the delivery of a LDV campervan, they would run me to the British Car Auctions in Glasgow. The lady of the house was delegated the job, off we set in this Vauxhall Corsa, which was low on fuel, so she stopped at a filling station and was rummaging through the glove box, for a loyalty card, and pulled out a large knife, no sign of emotion she just said, "It's my son's car!" and I had to show her the way to the Auction house.

Again in Scotland, again an LDV, the majority of these LDV's were ex Royal Mail, as this one was. It had been purchased in Glasgow and delivered to Derby. It was then sold to a customer in Paisley, a few miles away from the auctions. Again the customer had agreed to run me back to the auctions, where I would collect a vehicle, for the return journey. So here I am in Paisley, at a nice row of semi-detached houses. I knocked on the door, a lady came out, looked at me and said "What do you want?" I was a little taken back by her appearance; she was sporting a beard, I explained the reason of being there; she said "He doesn't want it," "Sorry but it's paid for", I replied, "Well you said it's ex-Royal Mail, and its red," "Yes, all Royal Mail are Red," "No they are not, they are Green," her language was peppered with swear words, telling me to "Go away, her husband didn't want it, didn't need it, he had a car, it only needed a clutch."

Then thank goodness her husband turned up, she turned on him, "What do want it for?" he replied "It's nothing to do with you, it's for fishing trips" I thought let me get out of here, so eventually he did run me to the auctions, explaining that she had mental health problems. A thought had struck me that none of the neighbours or passing people had batted an eyelid.

For this tale I'm back in Southampton, this time the Port. I had delivered a van for export, and I'd walked to the Railway Station, arriving in time to see that the train had just pulled in. There wouldn't have been time to pay for a ticket at the office, so I approached an official at the barrier, and asked him, "If I could pay on the train?" he replied " No sorry", I said "Well no problem it's not straightforward anyway as I have a seniors rail card", plus I knew it was an hourly service. At this he said, "Come with me," it was only then that I noticed his badge, Senior Revenue Officer, he beckoned the train manager over, and told him that he had sanctioned it, and I could pay on the train, and that I was travelling to Derby changing at Birmingham.

The train manager said "Go to one of the first class carriages," he also said "It's a bit manic today, so don't worry I'll come to you when I can." We hadn't gone past Southampton Airport when he was collecting my fare, he kept his voice down, and telling me to stay in First Class, as really there was no other room on the train. He went on to explain that apparently this was the busiest day of the year, October half term, even busier than Christmas. As the train arrived at the stations, you could hear the stations tannoy, pleading with passengers to wait for the next train. At Reading two males boarded the same carriage as mine, they explained that they were travelling to Birmingham International, could they please upgrade to First Class? They had to pay an additional one hundred and sixty pound's each, don't forget they had already paid once, and this was a single journey.

I sat there thinking to myself, there's no way I would pay that kind of money, yes, the seats were comfortable, I thought that they must have more money than sense. Within minutes of leaving Reading, there came a couple of Ladies pushing a trolley, and they said to me, "Would Sir like any lunch?" I said "Well yes, but how much is it?" They looked at me smiling saying "There's no charge; you are First Class aren't you?" I said "Oh yes," so I enjoyed my lunch and then, they came around later with coffee and chocolate biscuits! Well I had paid thirty pound's. The passengers in first class were complaining that they couldn't get to the toilets, because there were so many people sitting on the floor and standing.

When we eventually arrived at Birmingham I said to the Train Manager, who was now my best mate, "Bet that's a relief," as a lot of people were leaving the train, he said "Not really, there's going to be a further delay here, as due to the crowded conditions a passenger has collapsed and we have to await the paramedics."

I wished him well, and managed to get a seat on my connection, again this train was packed. This time my travelling companion was actually a Train Driver, in conversation with him, he told me he was a Freight Train Driver. In response to my questions he told me about the job, he said that the biggest problem they faced was suicides. Some drivers could get over it, but others couldn't, and when he told me that the salary, was over thirty thousand pound's, I asked if they were recruiting. I could tell he thought I was too old, but I was enquiring for my son. Again he surprised me when he said quite a few of the drivers were ex graduates, as indeed he was.

Let's travel down the country to South Wales, a beautiful part of the U.K. to Newport, only this time to collect a vehicle. It was a little Bedford Rascal (you know one of those like a dog kennel on wheels). As was often the case it was a non-starter due to a flat battery, no problem, quick jump off the auction houses jump leads, and it's running. I checked the fuel gauge, it said half a tank, so off I set. After a few miles I came to a Transport Café, the petrol gauge had gone down a considerable way, so I drove to the top of the lorry park, which was on a downhill gradient. I switched the engine off to remove the petrol cap, and then went to start up again, no go, still flat battery.

I rolled it down the lorry park to jump start it, no joy, so I rolled it onto the fuel pumps and filled up. I then approached a lorry driver and asked "Am I o.k. for a snatch?" which he readily agreed. He secured a rope from my van to the rear of his trailer, and sure enough my van started, the trouble was, it pulled off the rear stabiliser bars from the back of his trailer! I couldn't believe that my mobile dog's home could do so much damage; I mean his spare wheel was nearly as big as my van.

I apologised to the driver and gave him a fiver, saying that I hoped he wouldn't get into trouble, he replied "Don't worry mate, my second name is trouble, I'm always in it."

Let's go back to Scotland again, and my last job for Ivan, he rang me and asked if I would deliver a pickup truck to Aberdeen, I said "Yes, but not in a day," "No problem Bill, I'll book you a flight back," so it was arranged for the following Friday, actually that was the first day we could get a flight from Aberdeen to East Midlands Airport. I did a job on the Tuesday to somewhere in Kent, and asked for the Aberdeen delivery address, Ivan's response was "I'll text it through to you," but he didn't, nothing new there.

The flight was booked for 19.30 hours, on midday on the Thursday I rang Ivan again asking for the address, "Yes I'll text you," I told Ivan "that it was a tight schedule to meet especially to meet the flight timetable," but again as was the norm, the vehicle still had work to be done it. So, it was arranged that he would meet at 7am on the Friday morning, this time he did text the guy's number to me. I rang the customer and told him that I would be arriving the following day, and also reminded him that he would give me a lift to the Airport, in general conversation he asked me "Which way I would be coming?" "I explained about the 7am start, and I would be coming up the M1, A1 to Newcastle on Tyne, then cut across country to Edinburgh", his comments were, "It's cutting it a bit fine, I originate from Newcastle," I did explain that I had been to his part of the country before," at that he gave me his address and post code.

Within minutes I was back on the phone to him, querying his postcode, he repeated it, "yes, it was correct," I said "But that's Inverness! Not Aberdeen," Ivan's geography again, only this time it's a proper 'cock up'. I rang Ivan and arranged that I would collect the truck that afternoon, so that I would be able to make an even earlier start the next morning. I did ask the customer if he would still take to the airport, the answer of "No" was not unexpected; it was after all one hundred and twenty miles away. But now I have a new deadline, in order to get to Aberdeen in time I would have to catch a train departing Inverness at 15.20. I set off very early about 5am, with a flask of hot water and a jar of coffee. Toilet stops were taken at the roadside, or at my frequent refuelling stops.

The pick up truck was an LDV petrol/gas conversation motor; I arrived in Inverness with 15 minutes to spare, wow made it! I sat back to enjoy the ride, my station was called Dyce, I had asked how far away the station was from the Airport, and was told at both Inverness and by the Train Manager, about a mile, so I'd got plenty of time. As we approached Dyce, I suddenly realised that I had still got hot water in my flask, again thinking of airport security relating to liquids, I decided to get rid of it, so I emptied it onto the floor, down by my feet. It was at this moment that they came past me with the refreshment trolley, I saw them looking at me, as I sat there with steam rising from my feet area, and we can guess what they were thinking.

On arrival at Dyce station, I approached a taxi driver on the rank, asking him for directions; he said "It's a bit complicated," "But it's only a mile" I said, he replied "Yes if you walk over that way," pointing in the distance." I looked perplexed, at which he explained, "Yes, it's only a mile away if you were to walk over the runway." He quoted me ten pound's and agreed to stop at a cash point, so by now you think my troubles are over, wrong. Aberdeen Airport has a very nice setup, the airline you are flying with, in my case, Eastern Airways, has it's own departure lounge with free hot and cold drinks, and free biscuits, which were very well received. It was then announced that my flight had a delay of forty minutes, so at that I decided to ring Richard another sub-contractor to Ivan.

But first let me tell you of the arrangements that had been made. Richard was to collect me from the airport, because when I'd collected the truck I had left my car with Ivan, who because he was going to Norway on a skiing weekend, was delivering my car to Richards house, is that clear? Anyway on receipt of my call Richard sounded surprised to hear from me, and went on to tell me that my car was not at his house, and that Ivan must have forgotten. I thought what the hell am I going to do, how am I going to get from the airport and how am I going to collect my car? Richard did pick me up, but I had to borrow his car and then return it early the following day. So I'd set off at about 5am, it was 23.00 when I got home, an eighteen hour day. I was then back out of bed at 7am, and back to Richard's house in Derby to collect my car and home again for lunch time. It was another five hours for nothing, are you surprised that I refused to do any more jobs for Ivan. As I said in the beginning Ivan himself is a great bloke but his geography and organising skills left a lot to be desired.

Job 50 School Minibus Driver at Wardle Transport,
Well folks we have now nearly come to the end of my working life, and I only did this job, because it was my son who was in charge. The actual job, which with a guide was collecting handicapped children, was very rewarding, not financially, but spiritually. To see what some of these children had to cope with, and would still be suffering throughout their lives, yet still greet you with smiles and giggles was reward in itself, and makes you appreciate not only your own health, but your children, grandchildren and in my case great grandson. Before I say farewell, a couple of times I did a job for the WRVS, this was collecting old folks from a centre in Blurton, and returning them to their homes.

There was one old lady, aged ninety three, a bit confused or should I say 'a lot.' I stopped outside her house, and helped her down the steps, at which she said "Mind the dog," as we were walking up the path, I asked her about her dog, she said, "What dog, I haven't got a dog." Another time, but this time as I helped her off the bus, I noticed that the front door to her old folk's bungalow was damaged; she said "Somebody had done it in the night." I thought what a rotten society we live in, to do that to an old frail woman, well, in my opinion they wanted shooting, and said so to her, she agreed, as we got to the front door, her daughter opened it, I said to her "Your Mum's just been telling me about the door," her daughter said "Yes, she had a fall in the night and we had to break down the door to get in."

The lady involved in the previous tales had died, and this time I had a new lady on board, as was the custom if they knew where they lived they would say "I'm next," they weren't always right, but that's something else. I had done my drops around Blurton, and I was now in Dresden, a voice said "Driver when are you going to Blurton?" It was the new lady, I said "Were do you live?" She didn't know, so I rang the office, and they gave it to me, fortunately I knew where this address was, so back to Blurton, pulled up outside the address I had been given, "No I don't live here!" I double checked, yes, I was at the right place, eventually after much coaxing she went to the door, still not believing me, surprise, surprise the key opened the door.

The other occasion involved the early run, taking them in; I had collected the first lady in Longton, and went to the second pickup, in the Meir. As we were waiting, the lady said "What's that?" I looked and I couldn't see anything unusual, "What" I replied. She said "That" pointing at a cat", I said "A cat," "Oh what's a cat?" "It's one of them" I said still pointing at the cat, she asked "What do you feed them on?" "Cat food" was the answer, "What is it again?" "A Cat" I replied, she said it was outside my house, it's followed me. I said "Yes," thinking it must be turbo powered, and then saying a silent prayer for my pick up to hurry up, which was answered, the second lady came out, and the cat was forgotten about.

Job 51. On Line sex shop

To say that this was job number fifty one and my last job, is not strictly true, the era was a few years ago, it was when Tina was still at University. So I hear you ask, why the mystery; well the on- line shop, was in fact a sex shop. Me and a friend, Ian went into partnership; we both put in two thousand pound's, and I registered an internet domain name, www.sex4you.org.uk and we bought a ready made site complete with suppliers. What neither, Ian nor I, had imagined was the time and effort it took in maintaining the site.

The arrangement we had was that Ian would look after the computer end of the business, and I would look after the orders and the dispatching of the goods. This led to the first problem; neither Linda nor I could understand what half the items listed in the illustrated catalogue, actually were or what they did!

Through Ian's contacts, Staffordshire University were engaged to maintain the sites pages, this was a necessity as stock changed weekly, also Ian's other businesses bankers, Barclays, were approached to handle the financial end of the business. A meeting was arranged at the banks offices, which we both attended. Ian was embarrassed to find that the designated business manager, was a female, and if I remember correctly she was called Tracy.

On our arrival we were met and taken to her office, when I say office, it was a desk within an office, coffee was supplied, and all went well, until the question of what were we actually dealing in, Ian's answer was "Adult matters," mine was more straightforward, "Sex toys" Tracy, to be fair looked amused, however, you could hear the ripple of giggles from the surrounding desks. After careful consideration we both decided that it was a 'no go'. Ian could not spare the time element, and me, well, I was just bewildered and shall we say "Blinded by science."

Before I say goodbye I'll tell you about a couple of business opportunities that I didn't get involved in, the first one was back in the days of being a Market Trader, and being truthful I could see the scheme making money. But it was the ethics of the scam that bothered me, if it failed and gathered adverse publicity I had to consider the impact on my family, so I didn't take it any further, after telling you this I better explain what it was about. To make it legal you had to have at least two articles for sale, in this instance, the articles being Blow up Sex Dolls, they had to be quality ones, and expensive. I think at the time they were about £65.00 each, as long as you had these in your possession it was legal to offer them at what ever price you deemed fit.

Now this is where the scam came in, you targeted an area, offering these dolls at a bargain price of £25.00, your advert would give an accommodation address. On receipt of the cheque you would bank it, and send them a receipt and thank you letter stating that due to over whelming demand their goods would be dispatched within the next two–three weeks. After this period you would again write to them expressing your dismay that the supplier could not meet your order, so please find enclosed our cheque valued at £25.00, this is where the con was, on the back of the cheque in bright red ink, it was clearly marked SEX TOY. It was claimed that 90% of people would not present the cheque for payment.

The other business proposition involved minibuses, this was another bus operator, Gerry Buchanan. He called me one day to discuss his latest business, which was minibus conversions. He claimed he was buying Ford Transit vans that were accident damaged, then converting them into 12 seater minibuses. On the face of it, it looked good, and I did express interest in the project, however the more I listened to him, and took mental notes, I formed the opinion that something was not quite right! So I refused, boy was I right he got four years in jail, the bloke who did go in with him, got 2 years.

Epilogue

Now you've read my story, I hope you will agree with me that when the good Lord decides to take me, that I have had an amazing life. A Mother who the title/expression, "The Worlds Best Mum" richly deserved. Linda my long suffering wife, who has never agreed with any of my business proposals but has always not only backed me, but has worked alongside of me so together we did and have achieved a long and happy marriage. Let's not forget our children, Tracy, Keith & his wife

Tracy, Tina and all their wonderful children, Daniel, Sophie, Katie, Beckie, Kayleigh, and great grandson Jake, plus of course, my son in law Steve. Finally let's not forget all the people who have either had the pleasure, or the misfortune of working with me, or for me.

Love you all, Good bye,

13523486R00157

Printed in Great Britain
by Amazon.co.uk, Ltd.,
Marston Gate.